How to Read Faces

By the same author
Fortune-Telling by Astrology
Fortune-Telling by Palmistry
Fortune-Telling with Numbers
The ESP Workbook

HOW TO READ FACES

Rodney Davies

THE AQUARIAN PRESS

First published 1989

British Library Cataloguing in Publication Data
Davies, Rodney
How to read faces
1. Physiognomy
I. Title
138

ISBN 0-85030-804 6

*The Aquarian Press is part of the Thorsons Publishing Group,
Wellingborough, Northamptonshire, NN8 2RQ, England*

Printed in Great Britain by Woolnough Bookbinding Limited,
Irthlingborough, Northamptonshire

1   3   5   7   9   10   8   6   4   2

CONTENTS

Men's proper business in this world falls mainly into three divisions:
First, to know themselves, and the existing state of the things they have to
do with.
Secondly, to be happy in themselves, and in the existing state of things.
Thirdly, to mend themselves, and the existing state of things, as far as
either are marred and mendable.

From *Man's Business in Life* by John Ruskin.

INTRODUCTION

'Every one is in some degree a master of that art which is generally distinguished by the name of Physiognomy; and naturally forms to himself the character or fortune of a stranger, from the features and lineaments of his face.'

From the *Spectator*, No. 86 (1711) by Addison.

The interpretation of a face, as Joseph Addison suggests, is something that we all do to a certain extent every time we meet someone new, and indeed our emotional reaction can on occasion be so powerful that we 'fall in love at first sight'. Other faces can just as strongly repel or even frighten us, although the majority perhaps leave us largely unmoved. Such natural analysis is reflected in the number of references in everyday speech to those facets of character supposedly linked with particular facial features, like the 'intelligent forehead', the 'inquisitive nose', the 'kind eyes', the 'sensuous lips', the 'cruel mouth', and the 'weak chin', which show that face reading, or physiognomy, is possibly as widely practised today as it was in the past.

Yet although we all intuitively read faces, the study of physiognomy as a proven method of understanding character and temperament has been largely neglected in recent years by both scientists and fortune-tellers. This has happened because the scientists have become increasingly fearful of investigating anything that smacks of superstition, whilst those involved in the 'occult' have shunned face reading because it seems 'too scientific', a position that was encouraged by those physiognomists who sought acceptance by the scientific community. For example, the well-known, turn-of-the-century face reader Annie Oppenheim, F.B.P.S., claimed that 'physiognomy must not be confounded with palmistry, thought-reading, or astrology, and it has nothing whatever to do with foretelling future events or divining the past. It is simply the art of reading character from a person's face—to be able to tell, according to the shape of the head and the form of the features, what those features denote'.

But now a wind of change is blowing through both these opposite camps. Scientists have become bolder, to the extent that some are willing to investigate such 'dangerous' subjects as palmistry, thought-reading, and astrology, and those who practise these fortune-telling methods have increasingly welcomed the positive results that the scientists have sometimes achieved.

I have therefore written this book in the hope that it will stimulate fresh interest in a study that can be of benefit to everyone. For face reading is a method of character analysis and fortune-telling that is not only as ancient and exact as palmistry and astrology, but can also enable you to understand your own character and fate, and that of your loved ones, friends and enemies, as well as the people to whom you sit opposite on the bus and train.

Finally, to avoid the text becoming laboured I often use the pronouns 'he', 'his' and 'him'; these should of course be taken to refer to both sexes.

Chapter One

THE HISTORY OF FACE READING

'Man is read in his face; God in his creatures.'

From *Deus in Creaturis* by Ben Johnson.

The interpretation of character and fate from the study of a person's face is so old that we can neither give it a place of origin nor an accurate date of birth. It is probably as old as man and may well have arisen spontaneously among different tribal and racial groups, which is why no culture can claim it for its own. Thus face reading was ancient when man first began seeking guidance from both the stars and from the lines on his hands.

Human beings have always looked at each other's faces, and such contemplation must have soon led to the general supposition that the face symbolizes the inner man or woman. There is nothing magical or mysterious about this. After all, most faces are unique to their owners and therefore represent his or her character and temperament. And when it was realized that similar facial features betray similar traits of character, the time was necessarily ripe for physiognomy to be systematized into a method of character analysis and, later, of divination.

But for those who perhaps doubt that the face can accurately reveal character, let alone fate, I can do no better than ask them to consider the evidence provided by identical twins, who share identical facial features and, as research has shown, near identical patterns of behaviour. And even more remarkable is the fact that their lives often run parallel to one another, sometimes to the extent of them sharing the same experiences.

For instance, when Americans Ester Pauline and Pauline Ester Freidman were children they were inseparable. The twins not only talked alike and dressed alike, but when they married they shared a double wedding. Later they both became journalists specializing in the solving of problems, and today their columns are syndicated in hundreds of newspapers across the United States, where they are better known under their by-lines of Abigail Van Buren—of Dear Abby fame—and Anne Landers.

But even more startling and convincing are the remarkable cases of parallel development shown by identical twins that have been raised apart from one another. For while we can perhaps accredit similar character traits and life experiences to a shared upbringing, such is not the case with twins who have been separated from one another since early childhood.

Jim Lewis and Jim Springer are two American identical twins who were adopted by different families within weeks of their birth and who lived entirely separate lives for the following 37 years. Hence they were amazed to discover when they finally met up with one another, that not only had they developed identical characters and tastes, but that the pattern of their lives had mirrored one another's to a remarkable degree.

Both, for example, chain-smoke the same brand of cigarette, drink the same brand of beer, drive the same make of car, bite their finger- nails down to the quick, enjoy mathematics and stock-car racing but dislike baseball and spelling, and leave love-notes lying around their homes for their wives. Each twin has also suffered two heart attacks, is troubled by insomnia and haemorrhoids, and by evening migraine headaches which began when they were 18 years old. They have both had vasectomies.

Even more surprisingly, both men once worked as garage atten- dants and for the MacDonald hamburger chain, and had become part-time deputy sheriffs. Both had married and divorced a woman named Linda, and had subsequently married one named Betty. Jim Lewis had christened his first son James Alan, while Jim Springer had named his son James Allen. Both men have a dog named Tony. They also spend their vacations with their families at the same beach in Florida, although at different times of the year.

British identical twins Roy and Paul Wells were parted as babies when their parents separated and were brought up 9,000 miles apart, Roy being taken to New Zealand by his father, while Paul remained in England with his mother, who later remarried. It wasn't until 22 years later, in 1981, that Roy returned to England and sought out Paul, who soon found himself remarking, 'It's as if an emotional void has been filled. We're exactly the same.'

Indeed, their tastes and attitudes are disturbingly alike. Neither twin likes vegetables or getting up in the morning, and both hate spiders. Both are allergic to dust and have suffered from asthma.

Their favourite colour is blue, their favourite animals are lions and tigers, and they prefer documentaries to other television programmes. They feel most comfortable in light-coloured casual clothes, choose white wine in preference to red, and both want to visit America and India. Their tastes in women run to independent-minded blondes who do not use make-up, and they both one day want to have two children and live in a large house. Both also recalled that the saddest time in their lives happened when they were 15 years old.

Canadian identical twins Margaret Judson and Marion Smith met up by accident in a Toronto department store after having been separated and out of touch for 21 years. It didn't take them long to discover that they had both taken piano lessons and sung alto in their respective church choirs; that they had developed into expert roller-skaters and had considered turning professional; that they had had their tonsils removed in the same year; and that they had both married sailors of the same age, build and weight, who had been at sea for four years. And while Margaret, unlike Marion, had been in the army, Marion had tried to enlist but had been rejected.

Identical twins frequently live to the same age and very often die within days of each other, sometimes on the same day. For instance, New York gynaecologists and identical twins Cyril and Stewart Marcus were found dead on the same day, in different parts of the city, both having committed suicide by taking an overdose of barbiturates. Yet their deaths were entirely unrelated. Likewise, in 1952, two 90-year-old identical twin sisters were found lying half-starved among huge piles of hoarded newspapers in their Greenwich Village apartment. They were rushed to hospital, where they died within hours of each other. And in 1962 another pair of identical twin sisters passed away within minutes of one another, at the North Carolina mental hospital where they had been undergoing treatment for schizophrenia. On the night in question they were sleeping in different parts of the hospital, so that they could not have known by ordinary means what was happening to the other.

Such examples could be multiplied, but one does not need to labour the point. What is evident is that the faces of identical twins accurately reflect their similarity of temperament and taste and the parallel nature of their lives. This is particularly true of identical twins that have been separated, as those who have been brought up together often strive to be different and thereby acquire a consciously nurtured independence.

Common experience also tells us that unrelated people who happen to look alike share similar traits of character. In fact it has often been remarked that married couples who live harmoniously together and who share common interests, gradually develop a remarkable similarity of face and form, to the extent that they are sometimes mistaken for brother and sister. In this respect they conform to the basic tenet of physiognomy, which is 'as without, so within'.

A systematized approach to the interpretation of facial features can be said to have originated in the West with the philosophical speculations of Empedocles, who lived at the Greek colony of Acragas in Sicily in the fifth century BC. His ideas about the nature of the world were applied to mankind, whose character they helped explain, and in turn linked man's inner state to his outer form.

Empedocles was a truly remarkable man, a type whom we would today call an eccentric genius. For apart from being an original thinker, poet, orator, physician and statesman, he was also a mystic and a miracle-worker, who believed that his knowledge gave him the power to control nature, to the extent of being able to raise the dead. He accepted the doctrine of the transmigration of souls, and maintained that the souls of sinners were condemned to occupy one mortal body after another until they became sufficiently purified to escape from the material world altogether. He became convinced that he was living through his last incarnation, having previously existed as 'a boy and a girl, a beast and a bird and a dumb fish in the sea', and to make sure that his soul went off to the realm of the gods, he committed suicide in 430 BC by jumping into the fiery volcanic cone of Mount Etna. He outlined his somewhat odd ideas in a long poem titled *Purifications*, of which fragments still survive. Aristotle acknowledged him as the inventor of rhetoric, without which no Greek could hope to advance himself, and Galen called him the father of Italian medicine.

Empedocles' philosophical speculations, however, were set down in his poem *On Nature*, which was widely read and highly influential. In it he claimed that ultimate reality consists of four 'root-substances' or elements, the now familiar Fire, Air, Water and Earth, which are indestructible and everlasting. These, by combining together in different proportions, created the world and everything in it, which naturally includes ourselves. They are moved, said Empedocles, by two forces: Love, which attracts them together, and Strife, which drives them apart. Hence Love and Strife are responsible for the flux of the world, eternally building things up and breaking them down. A modern physicist would doubtlessly refer to them as attraction and repulsion.

Such ideas were taken an important step further by Hippocrates of Cos (*c.* 460–377 BC), the 'father of medicine', who postulated that the four elements manifest within the human body as the four life-giving liquids or 'humours', which in turn determine a person's temperament and physique. Thus Air, which is moist and hot, forms blood;

Fire, which is dry and hot, forms yellow bile; Earth, which is dry and cold, forms black bile; and Water, which is moist and cold, forms phlegm. Hippocrates said that when the four humours were present in someone's body in equal amounts, the result was good health, an equable temperament, and a poised or balanced physique. But when one occurred in excess, the internal environment was put out of balance, which resulted in specific health problems, a particular temperamental bias, and certain physical peculiarities. Thus a person with a surfeit of blood demonstrated a *sanguine* temperament and physical type; of yellow bile, a *choleric* temperament and physique; of black bile, a *melancholic* temperament and physique; and of phlegm, a *phlegmatic* temperament and physique.

The sanguine type is perhaps the most fortunate of the four, as he is generally easy-going, optimistic, humorous, amorous, and intelligent, while the choleric type, who is distinguished by his energy, irascibility, and aggression, is the most explosive. The phlegmatic type is essentially placid and apathetic, being cool and calm, if not always collected, and the melancholic individual is, as the name suggests, sad, gloomy, and depressive.

The complexion and the other physical attributes are determined by the colour and fluidity of the principal humour. Thus the choleric person, for example, who has an excess of yellow bile or choler, is tall and thin, has a long, hatchet-jawed face, dark eyes and black hair, a skin with a yellow hue, and whose physical weaknesses derive from his liver insufficiency, which makes him bilious. And while he is excitable and easily-angered, his mood can quickly crash, leaving him sad and despondent.

As time went by it became plain that not everybody fell completely into one or other of the four temperament and physical groupings outlined by Hippocrates, but that most of us are mixtures with less starkly defined temperaments and physical attributes. Thus John Aubrey in his *Brief Lives* remarks of the philosopher Thomas Hobbes (1588–1679), that 'from forty, or better, he grew healthier, and then had a fresh, ruddy complexion. He was *sanguineo-melancholicus*; which the physiologers say is the most ingenious complexion.'

The first written work on physiognomy that we know of came from the pen of Aristotle (384–322 BC), a former pupil of Plato and tutor to Alexander the Great, although by no means all scholars are convinced that *Displaying the Secrets of Nature Relating to Physiognomy* was written by him. The book is divided into six chapters, and deals with physiognomy in its widest sense, describing the meaning of all parts of the human body, from the head to the feet. It is an important work, not because it is particularly deep or inspiring, but because it is the base upon which Western physiognomy was erected and upon which it was maintained for over two thousand years. Indeed, the writings of most of the later physiognomists are little more than re-workings of Aristotle, bereft as they are of original thought or independent observation.

It was Aristotle, interestingly enough, who added another element to the four postulated by Empedocles, which he named Ether and which he imagined to be divine and incorruptible. In *De Mundo* the great philosopher tell us 'then five elements, situated in spheres in five regions, the less being in each case surrounded by the greater—namely, Earth surrounded by Water, Water by Air, Air by Fire, and Fire by Ether—make up the whole universe. All the upper portion represents the dwelling of the gods, the lower the abode of mortal creatures.'

But Aristotle does not go on to suggest that this means that there are five human temperaments or that the human soul is made of Ether, which he might reasonably have done. Indeed, I mention Aristotle's fifth element only because his hypothesizing closely parallels that of the Chinese, who were developing their own theory of the Five Elements at about this time, as well as a system of physiognomy which has persisted, with a number of important additions, right down to the present day.

This apparently coincidental link with the Chinese occurs again at the end of *De Mundo*, when Aristotle says, 'God being one has many names, being called after all the various conditions which he himself inaugurates. We call him Zen and Zeus, using two names in the same sense, as though we should say "him through whom we live".' The name Zen derives from the Greek ζην, meaning 'to live'. In China there later flourished an important Buddhist sect called Ch'an, which we know better nowadays by its Japanese name 'Zen', meaning 'meditation'. Zen Buddhism differs from ordinary Buddhism by placing special emphasis on meditation as a way of obtaining enlightenment and by turning its back on the reading of the scriptures. Zen became popular with the Japanese Samurai, whereby it mirrored the martial prowess and conquering spirit of Aristotle's most famous pupil, Alexander the Great.

Before we leave the Greeks it is worth mentioning that Aristotle's celebrated forbear Socrates (470–399 BC) was a talented physiognomist. We know from Plato that he predicted the rise of Alcibiades from the markings in his face, and Apuleius tells us that Socrates divined the extraordinary talents of Plato at their first meeting from his face and general bearing. Even more unusual is the story regarding a physiognomist named Zopyrus, who, upon viewing Socrates' features, pronounced him to be stupid, sensual and dull, and that Socrates agreed with him, saying that this had indeed been his nature until it had been rectified by the study of philosophy.

We know from the writings of Juvenal, Pliny, Suetonius and others, that physiognomy was popular among the Romans. Suetonius records, for example, that a certain physiognomist, whom he does not name, was once summoned to read the face and predict the fate of Britannicus, the handsome and popular son of the current emperor Claudius, whose successor he was assumed to be. The physiognomist carefully examined Britannicus, and then, to everybody's astonishment, announced that the young man would not succeed his father, 'whereas Titus (who happened to be present) would achieve that distinction'. And that's exactly what happened. Britannicus was poisoned by Nero, who was in turn deposed by the ageing Galba, who was successively followed by Otho, Vitellius, and Vespasian, until at last Titus was made emperor. Suetonius remarks of Titus, that 'though not tall, he was graceful and dignified, both muscular and handsome, except for a certain paunchiness.'

The only problem with this story is that it is virtually identical to the one told about the young Octavius, even though it is by means of astrology, not physiognomy, that the future is revealed. Apparently Octavius once paid a visit with his friend Agrippa to the well-known astrologer Theogenes. The latter first cast Agrippa's chart, from which he predicted a remarkable public career for him. Hearing this, Octavius declined to supply Theogenes with his birth data, fearing that his future prospects would not be as favourable. However, he was at last persuaded to do so, whereupon Theogenes cast his chart and immediately divined that he was destined for greatness. In fact he was so awed by what he saw that he flung himself at the future emperor's feet. And he was correct, for Octavius in due course assumed the purple and took the name Augustus. Astronomically-minded readers may care to note that Octavius (or Augustus) was born in 63 BC on 23 September, a birthday which he coincidentally shared with one of the Renaissance's most celebrated physiognomists Gerolamo Cardano, of whom more later.

The works of two Roman physiognomists have come down to us, although both sets of writings are broadly Aristotelian in content and viewpoint. Yet those of Polemon, who flourished in the middle of the second century AD, do deal with the nature and the physical attributes of the four temperament types in unusual depth, while one of the two books penned by Adamantius, a Jew who converted to Christianity, examines with some originality the meaning of eye expressions.

Following the fall of the Roman Empire, the continent of Europe entered into a cultural vacuum known as the Dark Ages, which persisted until a fresh lamp was burned in Renaissance Italy. During this long and forbidding period the ancient texts covering the whole field of human knowledge were either lost or forgotten, and so went largely unread, except in the monasteries, where great efforts were made to carry on with the tradition of learning and scholarship. Hence little was added to the extant works on physiognomy, particularly as its study, like that of palmistry, astrology and other 'occult' practices, was regarded as pagan superstition and therefore of the devil.

Fortunately, however, the Arabs were not so strictured, and it is believed that physiognomy was widely employed by them as a method of understanding human character and fate. Certainly Marco Polo (1254–1324) informs us in *The Travels* that Baghdad 'is a great centre for the study of the law of Mahomet and of necromancy, natural science, astronomy, and physiognomy'. Ali ben Ragel has left us a book on the meaning of birthmarks and moles, while Rhazes published a volume in 1040 that contains several chapters devoted to physiognomy. Likewise, the physician and philosopher Avicenna (980–1037) wrote about physiognomy at some length in *De animalibus*, although much of it is taken directly from Aristotle and from other Greek and Roman writers. The same may be said of those references to the subject made by Ibn Rushd or Averroes (1126–1198) in *De sanitate*, which he published in 1165.

Marco Polo also records that when on a visit to eastern India he noticed that 'there are many experts in the art called physiognomy, that is, the recognition of the characters of men and women, whether they be good or bad. This is done merely by looking at the man or woman'. However it was known by the Indians at a much earlier date that the outer person represented his or her inner condition, for we read in the *Svetasvatara Upanishad*, which was probably composed *c.* 500 BC, that 'the first signs of progress on the path of yoga are health, a sense of physical lightness, clearness of complexion, a beautiful voice, an agreeable odour of the person, and freedom from craving.' And even in Buddhist Tibet today, the reincarnated Dalai Lama is recognized by certain bodily signs, which are marks of his divinity.

The Chinese, as was mentioned earlier, developed a unique system of face reading in pre-Christian times, although it was probably based on physiognomical techniques introduced from India. There are many references to physiognomy in Chinese texts dating back as far as 300 BC, and indeed face reading has remained an important method of character analysis and divination among the Chinese right up to the present day. For example, one third century BC work records how the mandarin Ts'ai Tse visited a famous physiognomist, who examined him, laughed, and said: 'Sir, you have a big nose, thick eyebrows, high shoulders, a domineering air, and weak knees. I have heard it said that superior men do not consult physiognomists—why don't you follow their example?' To which Ts'ai Tse replied that although he possessed wealth and honour, he did not know how long he was going to live. 'Ah,' responded the diviner, 'then I can put your mind at rest. You have 43 years left ahead of you.' It was a prediction which of course made Ts'ai Tse very happy. And it came true!

The ancient doctrine of the Five Elements plays a central part in Oriental face reading, as these symbolize the five types of human being, which each have their own particular physical features, in the same way that the four Empedoclean elements came to represent the four types of Western man. The five Chinese elements are Fire, Earth, Water, Metal and Wood.

It is quite remarkable how the first three elements were shared by the East and West, as there was no possibility of a transfer of ideas from one culture to the other either prior to or during the lifetime of Empedocles, who died about 50 years before Alexander the Great and his army penetrated as far east as the upper reaches of the Indus river. Indeed, it seems entirely inexplicable.

Five was the magic number of the Chinese, who saw pentads (as I pointed out in my *Fortune-Telling with Numbers*) wherever they looked. The Chinese recognized five colours, five human senses, five odours, five tastes, five zones of space, five musical notes, five metals, five duties, five directions, five vital facial features—the ears, the eyebrows, the eyes, the nose, and the mouth—and a plethora of other fives too numerous to mention. Unfortunately lack of space does not allow for a more detailed consideration of the history and development of Chinese face reading, although certain aspects of the art will be dealt with in due course, notably with regard to foretelling the future.

The European Renaissance began in Italy during the fifteenth century, prompted into being as it was by the downfall of Constantinople (1453), which resulted in the arrival in Italy of Greek refugees who brought with them thousands of classical manuscripts, and by the invention of printing (1454), which allowed cheap copies of the translated works to be read by a wide and eager audience. Educated people were at last able to read the thoughts and ideas of Plato, Aristotle, Ovid, Horace, Pliny, Lucretius, Cicero and the like, models that sparked off a flowering of Italian genius, whose impetus spread throughout Europe, thus broadening men's minds and widening their vision, and which in turn translated itself into important advances in the fields of art, music, science, literature, philosophy, and economics.

It is not, therefore, surprising that this important period led to renewed philosophical speculation about the nature of man, and to an accompanying interest in those arts like astrology and physiognomy that offered a means to such understanding. And because these had been written about by Aristotle and other classical luminaries they gained attention despite the hostility of the Church.

Yet there had been a number of authors who wrote about face reading in pre-Renaissance times, although their works were not widely disseminated. For example, Albertus Magnus (1193–1280), the Bishop of Ratisbon, who was both a scholar and a scientist of distinction, as well as being a theologian, revealed how a face may be read in his *De animalibus*, although much of what he says was filched from Aristotle and Polemon. His contemporary, Michael Scot (*c.* 1175–1232), the so-called 'sage of Balwearie', also completed a physiognomical work titled *De hominis phisiognomun* while employed as court astrologer to Emperor Frederick II. Scot's opus became the first physiognomical book to be printed when it rolled off the presses in 1477, whereupon it became something of a best-seller. And the Italian doctor and alchemist Pietro d'Abano (1250–1316) likewise wrote a number of books on both astrology and face reading.

During the sixteenth century many physiognomical texts were published, which came from the pens of such obscure people as Pomponius Guaricus, Bartolomeo Cocles (who also wrote under the pseudonym 'Andrea Corvo'), Jean Taisier, Michael Blondes, Anselm Douxciel, Jean de Indagine, Gratarolus, Magnus Hund, and, best known of all, Gerolamo Cardano and Giovanni (or Giambattista) della Porta. The first printed work in English appeared in 1577. This was Dr Thomas Hill's *The Contemplation of Mankynde, contayning a singular Discourse after the Art of Physiognomie*, which was, however, largely derivative. The earliest original printed work in English is therefore the anonymous *A Pleasant Introduction to the Art of Chiromancie and Physiognomie* (1588).

It is time now to briefly consider the lives and works of the aforementioned Cardano and Porta, whose writings on physiognomy, which were both original and influential, are but a small part of their large and varied output.

Gerolamo Cardano, who is also known by his Anglicized name of Jerome Cardan and by his Latinized name Hieronymum Cardanum (or Hieronymus Cardanus), was a true Renaissance man. Born at Pavia, near Milan, Italy, on 23 September 1501, he not only became one of the period's greatest mathematicians—his *Ars Magna* is still consulted—but also, after Versalius, its greatest physician. His 83 books on medicine practically form a library by themselves, and they were accompanied by others on mathematics, astronomy, physics, theology, astrology, dream analysis, physiognomy, and gambling.

Cardano is distinguished by his belief that a person's character and fate are symbolized by the shape, lines and markings of his or her forehead, which he maintained could provide as much information to the perceptive observer as the birth chart. He wrote a total of 13 books on the art of metoposcopy or forehead reading, at which he was the acknowledged master, and some of his observations are considered in a later chapter.

We are fortunate in that Cardano left us a self-description in his autobiography, *De Vita Propria Liber* (The Book of My Life), which he completed shortly before his death in 1576. His likeness, taken from a painting made in his 68th year, is shown in Figure 1. He writes:

'I am a man of medium height . . . (with) a neck a little long and inclined to be thin, cleft chin, full pendulous lower lip, and eyes that are very small and apparently half-closed; unless I am gazing at something . . . Over the eyebrow of my left eye is a blotch or wart, like a small lentil, which can scarcely be noticed. The wide forehead is bald at the sides where it joins the temples . . . I have a fixed gaze as if in meditation. My complexion varies, turning from white to red. An oval face, not well filled out, the head shaped off narrowly behind and delicately rounded.'

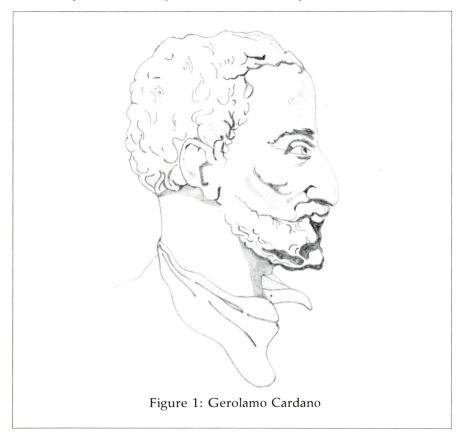

Figure 1: Gerolamo Cardano

Cardano unfortunately, and for no very clear reason, attempts to distance himself from his astrological and physiognomical studies in his autobiography, and warns that physiognomy

'is a long course and most difficult, one which requires exceptional pow- ers of memory and a very ready perception, which I scarcely believe are my endowment . . . I have discerned certain shadowy truths in it, but whether they are actually truths, or deceptions is very difficult to deter- mine, for you will be caught by deceptions simply because of the host of men and impressions, and their never-ending mutations'.

Giovanni Battista della Porta had little in common with the reclusive Cardano, for unlike his older fellow-countryman he was an outgoing, social man, who successfully combined his scientific pursuits with an interest in the arts. Born in Naples in 1538, and where he also died in 1615, Porta became the founder of the Academica dei Segretti, con- ducted experiments into physics and optics, about which he wrote a number of important books, took up gardening and developed it into an art, penned a series of highly successful stage comedies, and investigated several esoteric practices such as magic and astrology. In fact his best known work is *Magia naturalis* or Natural Magic.

In 1586 Porta published *De humana physiognoma* (The Physiog- nomy of Man), in which he compares the likenesses of people to cer- tain animals, thereby developing the thesis that if someone resem- bles an animal either wholly or in part (e.g. by having long ears), he or she would necessarily resemble that animal to a greater or lesser degree in temperament. This was by no means a novel idea, for not only had primitive man recognized a quasi-mystical connection between himself and the animals with which he shared the forests and savannas, but it had been commented upon by Aristotle and other writers, to the extent that it had become common knowledge. The great seventeenth century physician Sir Thomas Browne (1605– 1682) put the matter plainly in his *Christian Morals*. He said:

'We often observe that men do most act those creatures, whose constitu- tions, parts, and complexion do most predominate in their mixtures. This is a corner-stone of physiognomy, and holds some truth, not only in par- ticular persons, but also in whole nations. There are, therefore, provincial faces, national lips and noses, which testify not only to the natures of those countries, but of those which have them elsewhere.'

Yet Porta presented his views, which he illustrated with some strik- ing diagrams (see Figure 2), in the new, scientific manner, and his book quickly became a best-seller. Soon there was hardly an Italian aristocrat or a member of the expanding middle classes that had not

Figure 2: Illustrations from Porta's book showing the supposed
likenesses of men to certain animals

examined his (or her) face in the looking-glass to see if it was ovine, bovine, equine, porcine, feline, canine, or simply piscatorial.

People frequently do, of course, bear more than a passing resemblance to animals or birds, as Figure 3 graphically demonstrates, and those with such features often feel a strange affinity for the creature in question. How else can we explain the desire of Yehudi Menuhin, as he revealed to author Fleur Cowles in her book *People as Animals*, to be an eagle, David Jacobs an ape, Bernard Levin a cat, Jilly Cooper a mongrel dog, and Peter Ustinov a salamander?

But while an individual may resemble a cat, dog or whatever, can we really agree with Sir Thomas Browne that 'whole nations' have such likenesses? After all, while I have no difficulty in picturing Jacques Chirac or Francois Mitterand sitting at the side of a garden pond, would I be right to claim that every French national looks like a frog? These supposed national resemblances to animals were openly

Figure 3: Wildlife nurses Yvonne and Louise Veness with their charges

explored by an American doctor James W. Redfield in his book *Comparative Anatomy*, published in 1852.

Redfield commences this work, which has nothing to do with medical anatomy, by noting the similarity between some famous people and certain animals. He maintains, for example, that William the Conqueror, Oliver Cromwell, Robert Boyle, and Andrew Jackson resembled lions; that Anne of Cleeves, the fourth wife of Henry VIII, looked like a squirrel; and that Suraj-au-doula, the Hindu nawob who imprisoned 146 Englishmen and women in the Black Hole of Calcutta, was a rat in both facial appearance and nature.

He goes on to say:

'The animals which men in general have the greatest resemblance to are those they are most inclined to rear themselves upon, by either eating their flesh or riding upon their backs. Thus the resemblance is increased.'

And this is why Redfield rather strangely likens Laplanders to reindeer, Arabs to camels, Italians to horses, Spaniards to cocks, Greeks to sheep, Turks to turkeys, Persian to peacocks, the French to frogs, the Irish to dogs, Britons to oxen, Americans to polar bears, and Russians to Russian bears.

Warming to his subject, he continues:

'It is curious to trace the likeness between the Jews and the goat in the general appearance and in the features and expressions of the countenance. The signs of attack and relative defence in the convexity of the nose, the large signs of acquisitiveness and love of clothing in the breadth of that organ, the love of eminence in the elevation of the wing of the nostril, the want of concentration in the shortness of the upper lip, the strength of the love of the home and of family pride in the length and stiffness of the under lip, the energy and impulsiveness of love and will in the beard and chin, the signs of substitution, subterfuge, and the love of climbing, in the ridge of the eyebrow, the look of attention to external objects, and many other things, betray the relationship between the Israelite and the goat.'

The muscularity of the negro likens him most, in Redfield's opinion, to the elephant, although:

'the African tribes whose contentions furnish victims for the slave-trade are of the variety of negroes that are like fishes rather than elephants. Catching negroes is akin to fishing, and the caught are stowed away on board vessels like cod-fish and whale-oil; and were it not that they resemble fishes, and there is a feeling about this, and a dim perception of it, the business would be perfectly infernal.'

But Redfield admits that there is no clear division between those black people who resemble elephants and those who are generally piscatorial in appearance. He says:

'Of the class of negroes who resemble fishes, some are similar to whales, and these are akin to those who resemble elephants. Both are fond of *spouting*, as are the animals themselves, and this opens a channel for their ambitions to flow in . . . the negro distinguishes himself for his laugh as for his speechifying, and the stress which he lays upon the former shows that he attaches importance to it.'

Such nonsense did the art of physiognomy great harm, particularly as it had suffered badly from the attacks of natural philosophers in the eighteenth century, who were determined to root out anything that smacked of superstition. That it had survived at all was due largely to one man, the Swiss savant Johann Kaspar Lavater (1741–1801), who was blessed with an amazing intuitive talent for analysing men's character from their faces, and whose honesty, enthusiasm and natural charm speak so plainly from the pages of his published works. 'The perfect physiognomist,' he tells us, 'must unite an acute spirit of observation, a lively fancy, an excellent judgment, and, with numerous propensities to the arts and sciences, a strong, benevolent, enthusiastic, innocent heart; a heart confident in itself, and free from passions inimical to man.'

The reader may care to examine the self-portrait that Lavater included in his *Physiognomische Fragmente* (1778), about which he comments:

'A bad likeness of the author of these fragments, yet not to be absolutely mistaken. The whole aspect, especially the mouth, speaks inoffensive tranquillity, and benevolence bordering on weakness:—more understanding and less sensibility in the nose than the author supposes himself to possess—some talent for observation in the eye and eyebrows.'

But despite Lavater's interpretative ability, which was certainly great—and lack of space does not allow for any recitation of the stories regarding it—he was unable to add much that was new to the art of facial analysis. And science, which had already thrown out the soul, was intent on separating the mind from the body, by denying that the one had any effect upon the other. It was a stance that effectively neutered physiognomy's central thesis that the outer person symbolized the inner person, whose character and temperament could be read in his (or her) face and form. Hence Lavater was largely ignored by scientists, or derided by them as a harmless crank, and physiognomy became increasingly referred to as 'a supposititious

Figure 4: Johann Kaspar Lavater

method of determining character from the lineaments of the face'. The art was then almost squashed flat by phrenology, or head reading, which suddenly became, along with spiritualism, the 'in' psychic pursuit during the gas-lit years of the nineteenth century, when increasing numbers of people were crowding into the towns, eager for any entertainment that was new and different.

Phrenology was invented by the Viennese doctor Franz Joseph Gall (1758–1828), who claimed to have located a number of specific areas of the cranium whose development , or lack of it, reflected the underlying development of the brain, thereby revealing the character and mentality of the person concerned. It is ironic that Gall's discovery grew from his schoolboy observation that a particular facial feature always accompanied particular talents—he noticed, for example, that boys with good verbal memory possessed a wide space between their eyes— and that he went on to concentrate upon the geography of the cranium, rather than that of the face. He was also fortunate in gaining an energetic disciple in Johann Spurzheim (1776–1832), who by his writings and lecture tours abroad, spread the word about phrenology, most notably in the United States, where it was enthusiastically received.

But while phrenology was, and is, a department of physiognomy, it effectively diverted attention away from both face reading and from those other methods of analysing human character and fate from the body parts, such as palmistry. Yet if these were down, they were not out. Palmistry found its resurrectionist in Count Louis Hamon, better known as Cheiro, and face reading obtained an unexpected shot in the arm from the eminent criminologist Cesare Lombroso. It was a case of an Italian academic riding to the rescue of what was essentially an Italian art.

Chapter Two
THE CRIMINAL FACE, AND BODY TYPES

'A wise man will find us to be rogues by our faces: we have a suspicious, constrained countenance, often turning and slinking through narrow lanes.'

Jonathan Swift.

The criminal—or, rather, a certain type of criminal—has a distinctive face. An examination of its features will serve as a useful introduction to the art of face reading, and may help the astute reader from becoming unwittingly involved with the worst and most violent members of the criminal fraternity.

The investigation of the criminal's physiognomy was pioneered by Cesare Lombroso, the founder of the Modern or Positivist School of Criminology. Born in Verona, Italy, on 18 November 1835, Lombroso began work as an army physician, during which time he was 'struck by a characteristic that distinguished the honest soldier from his vicious comrade: the extent to which the latter was tattooed and the indecency of the designs that covered his body'.

On leaving the army in 1866, Lombroso took up the study of psychiatry, a field which, along with that of medical jurisprudence, was to absorb him for the rest of his life. He eventually and coincidentally became professor of psychiatry at the University of Pavia, the birthplace of Gerolamo Cardano, then the director of an insane asylum at Pesaro, and finally the professor of forensic medicine and psychiatry at the University of Turin. He was quick to realize:

'how necessary it was, in studying the insane, to make the patient, not the disease, the object of attention. In homage to these ideas, I applied to the clinical examination of mental alienation the study of the skull, with measurements and weights, by means of the esthesiometer and craniometer. Reassured by the result of these first steps, I sought to apply this method to the study of criminals.'

Lombroso was galvanized into action by the strange discovery he made within the skull of the notorious brigand Vilella, whose post-mortem examination he undertook. Upon opening the skull, he found a distinct depression, which he named the *median occipital fossa*, at the place where there is normally a bony ridge, and which was partnered by an enlargement of the vermis or upper spinal cord, both features being characteristic of the cranial interiors of rodents, apes and birds. He later wrote:

'At the sight of that skull I seemed to see all of a sudden, lighted up as a vast plain under a flaming sky, the problem of the nature of the criminal—an atavistic being who reproduces in his person the ferocious instincts of primitive humanity and the inferior animals.'

In other words, the criminal, or, more correctly, the congenital or born criminal, who as a group make up about a third of law-breakers, is a throwback to an earlier stage of human development, which was altogether more savage and bestial. And such beings, as Lombroso also discovered, are distinguished by specific outer marks or stigmata, as well as by certain traits of character. Hence Lombroso stumbled upon the truth which had been known for thousands of years by physiognomists, and which is well worth repeating—*as without, so within.*

The 'born criminal', whom Lombroso regarded as being morally insane, is unable to tell the difference between right and wrong, and may believe that his criminal actions are right and wholly justifiable. He does not possess a conscience and seldom, if ever, expresses regret for what he has done. He is a difficult and often violent child, a truant from school or, while there, a disruptive pupil, and who engages in petty crime at an early age and who then graduates to hooliganism and more serious crime, like shop-lifting, mugging and drug-dealing, in his teens. He typically lacks any emotional feeling for his fellow human beings, most notably his own family, although he often shows warmth towards total strangers and animals. He is lazy, impulsive, vindictive, boastful, cruel, and fond of vice and gambling. In these respects he accords in character with the Roman emperor Commodus, about whom the historian Aelius Lampridius remarks, that 'from his earliest boyhood he was base, shameless, cruel, lecherous, defiled in mouth too and debauched . . . He gave advance warning of his future cruelty in his twelfth year, at Centumcellae. For when he happened to have a bath in rather tepid water, he ordered the bath-keeper to be cast into the furnace'. And yet Commodus, like his equally debased predecessor Caligula, was kind to animals, as was the Nazi dictator Adolf Hitler.

Where his external self is concerned, Lombroso found that the born criminal usually displays certain of the following features:

- The face is disproportionally large when compared with the skull, neck, or body.
- The face is asymmetrical: the eyes and ears may be set at different heights, the nose is twisted or slants to one side, the mouth is uneven, etc.
- The forehead is narrow.
- The ears are abnormally large or stand out from the sides of the head. Or conversely, the ears may be undersized.
- The eyebrows are bushy and often meet above the nose.
- The jaw is strongly developed, frequently ape-like or prognathus.
- The nose slants upwards, revealing the nostrils.
- The beard is thin and patchy.
- The hair of the head is profuse and usually dark in colour, yet its direction of growth and tendency to form tufts, is abnormal.

The face shown in Figure 5 has several of the above-mentioned features. It belongs to Junzo Okudairo, a member of the Japanese

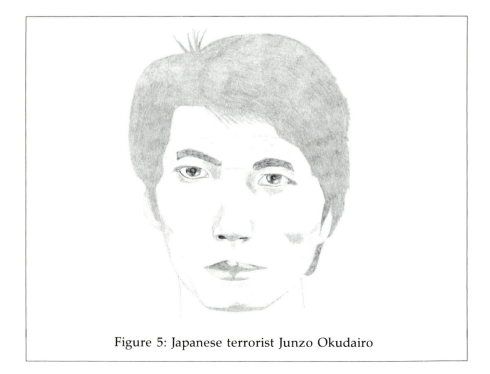

Figure 5: Japanese terrorist Junzo Okudairo

Red Army terrorist group, who is currently being sought by the police for having perpetrated a number of bomb outrages, the most recent of which, at the time of writing, took place at a US Navy nightclub in Naples, Italy, and which killed five people. He is also believed to be responsible for the bomb attacks carried out in June 1987 on the British and American embassies in Rome.

Okudairo's face is large compared to his overall head size, and an examination of his features reveals that his right eye and right eyebrow are respectively set on a higher level than those of the left. His nose has an asymmetrical twist to it, as does his mouth. His jaw and chin are strongly fashioned. His eyebrows are bushy—a feature, incidentally, that Lombroso noticed was common among murderers and rapists—and his forehead is narrow. The hair of the 40-year-old terrorist is thick and dark, and bears several upstanding tufts near the crown. There is no trace of a beard or moustache. His ears are not fully visible, although his right ear appears to be somewhat outstanding.

The man's face shows another negative feature that Lombroso failed to record, but which we now know to be highly significant. This is the upward 'floating' of the irises to reveal the white of the eye between them and the lower eyelids. Oriental physiognomists refer to this condition as *sanpaku* and claim that it symbolizes inner disharmony. It is also one sign of a violent and premature death, and which, combined with certain other negative features of Okudairo's face, indicates that he does not have long to live.

Okudairo does not, of course, regard himself as a common murderer, but rather as a brave volunteer fighting to liberate the oppressed peoples of the world. Yet his opinions and behaviour accord perfectly with those described by Lombroso as characterizing the born criminal. He believes his cause to be morally right and wholly justifiable; he is prepared to maim and murder in pursuit of his goals; and he has no regret for what he has done, even when innocent people have suffered at his hands. We are therefore right in branding him as a morally insane killer, who is in all probability psychotic.

Indeed, it is easy to understand why terrorist groups around the world are able to attract recruits, for they offer a supposedly legitimate way for the morally weak to give vent to their murderous instincts, while at the same time gaining the heroic admiration of those in the wider community who support their aims but who are less vicious. Every country produces thugs of this type, who, if they do not become criminals or terrorists, find a violent niche for themselves as secret policemen, torturers, hit-men and bodyguards.

The faces shown in Figure 6 are those of SS guards who served at

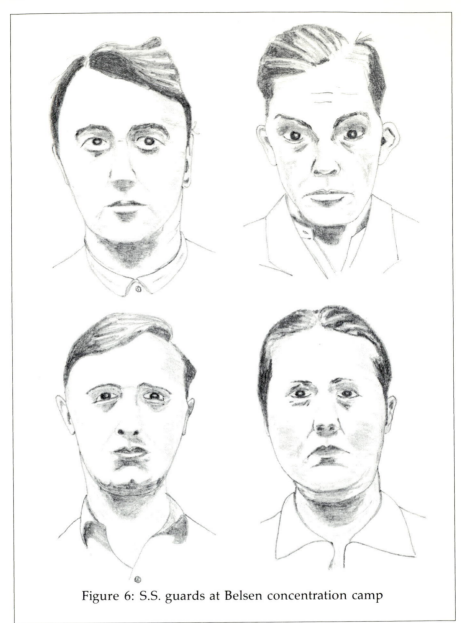

Figure 6: S.S. guards at Belsen concentration camp

the notorious Belsen concentration camp, where they whipped, beat, tortured and gassed those in their charge. No emotionally rational person could have participated in such acts without losing his or her sanity, yet these served the Reich with an apparently stoic cheerfulness, without conscience or regret. We might therefore classify them as morally insane, and it is fascinating to discover that their faces, with their asymmetries and other negative features, amply suggest the barrenness of their souls.

However, Lombroso acknowledged that the majority of criminals—about two-thirds—are not born to their trade, but enter it as a result of environmental influences. These he termed *criminaloid*. They are responsible, by and large, for the less serious types of crime, such as theft, fraud and forgery, although they may, on occasion, commit murder. They begin their criminal careers somewhat tentatively at a much later age than the born criminal. When arrested, they often not only admit their guilt but express genuine regret for what they have done. And because they possess some good qualities, they are capable of being reformed and returned to society.

Criminaloids frequently do not have the negative facial features which distinguish the born criminal, and if present they are usually found in a milder and less obvious form. Criminaloids also sometimes become prematurely grey or even go bald, which never happens to the born criminal. 'Forgers and swindlers,' noted Lombroso, 'wear a singular, stereotyped expression of amiability on their pale faces, which appear incapable of blushing and assume only a more pallid hue under the stress of any emotion. They have small eyes, twisted and large noses, and become bald and grey-haired at an early age, and often possess faces of a feminine cast.'

Lombroso was the first investigator to record that law-breakers tended to be shorter in stature than the average for their community, and that they have an arm-span measurement exceeding that of their height. His observations linking character with physiognomy were expanded by the German psychiatrist Ernst Kretschmer (1888–1964), who reported his findings to the world in his epoch-making work *Korperbrau und Charakter* (Physique and Character), published in 1921.

Kretschmer demonstrated a positive link, which had first been suggested by Hippocrates, between body and temperament. He recognized two extreme body types, the short, plump or *pyknic* person and the tall, slender or *asthenic* person, as well as two intermediate body types, the muscular *athletic* person and the physically mixed *dysplastic* person, so making four types which approximate in a general way to the four described by Hippocrates.

The pyknic person is below average height and has a rounded, podgy form, which typically grows in girth as he or she ages. His limbs are short, yet his movements are graceful. His large head bears a round, broad face with a small nose. His temperament is *cycloid*. That is, while he is normally extroverted, optimistic, easy-going and emotionally balanced, his mood can quickly change to one of unhappiness and depression, which is why the majority of manic-

Figure 7: Winston Churchill

depressives have a pyknic body build. He is prone to cancer and to disorders of the heart and circulatory system, including high blood pressure. It has since been shown that delinquents and criminals tend to be both pyknic in form and extroverted. Hence it comes as no surprise to learn that many tyrants and dictators, such as Nero, Napoleon Bonaparte and Benito Mussolini, are pyknic types. Winston Churchill (see Figure 7) is one example of a benevolent pyknic individual.

The asthenic, or leptosomatic, person has a long, narrow trunk and long, thin limbs, which typically gives him or her an above average height. He has a small head and an elongated, narrow and bony face with a large nose. He seldom becomes fat. His temperament is *schizoid*, which is to say he is introverted, quiet, shy and reserved, yet because his emotions are unstable, he tends to be nervous and excitable. The schizophrenic typically has an asthenic physique. He is prone to tuberculosis, diseases of the thyroid gland, and to nervous disorders, including insomnia and anxiety neurosis. He dislikes body-contact sports, yet he is well suited to and enjoys those sports where height is an advantage, such as basketball, those requiring patience and precision, like golf and snooker, as well as racket games and running.

The athletic person is marked out by his medium height, broad shoulders, narrow hips and developed musculature. Such people often have a large, angular face with a flattish nose and a strong jaw. Their temperament is essentially schizoid, and they are likely to suffer from the same sort of health disorders as the asthenic person. Their strength and disposition suits them for all kinds of manual work—they particularly enjoy working outdoors—as it does for those sports, like boxing, wrestling, shot-putting and weight-lifting, that are individual in nature. The current world heavyweight boxing champion, Mike Tyson, and the decathlete Daley Thompson, are classic examples of the athletic build.

Lastly, the dysplastic person possesses a mixed physique, which has elements found in the other three types, and also certain primitive or atavistic features, such as a small face and head, a low forehead, small or improperly formed ears, and a small nose. These people are by no means unintelligent, yet because they often lack inner balance and emotional maturity, they tend to be somewhat shiftless, impulsive and irresponsible. Indeed, they are basically schizoid in temperament and typically pursue a rather lonely path through the world. This is why many writers, poets, musicians, painters, avant-garde film makers and other artistic outsiders belong to this physical type.

Kretschmer's findings were later refined and largely substantiated by the American W.H. Sheldon, who invented three terms which have since passed into common usage to identify the three physical types that he described: the *endomorph*, the *ectomorph*, and the *mesomorph*. The first corresponds to Kretschmer's pyknic type, the second to his asthenic type, and the last to his athletic type. But unlike Kretschmer, Sheldon maintained that each of his three types had its own distinctive temperament, which he believed is associated with the body part that is emphasized.

The endomorph is *viscerotonic*, or social, by nature, the ectomorph is *cerebrotonic*, or intellectual, and the mesomorph is *somatotonic*, or physical. In this respect Sheldon was following in the footsteps of the French morphologists, who had earlier championed the linking of temperament with the most obvious body part. In this way they had identified the digestive, the thoracic, the musculo-articular, and the cerebral type of person.

Today far less attention is given to the linkage between temperament and physique by scientists and psychologists, chiefly because it has limited practical value. For while pyknic people, for example, are more likely to suffer from manic-depression than are those with a different physique, such knowledge does not help doctors to spot the people who will actually develop the disorder. And similarly, although it is true that 'born criminals' often display the physical features described by Lombroso, not every person with them necessarily becomes a criminal.

For what Lombroso did not realize is that even a 'bad' face can possess certain positive features, which symbolize inner qualities or strengths that can prevent its owner from turning into a criminal. I shall examine these and other traits, and explain how you can interpret your own face and those of others, throughout the rest of this book.

Chapter Three
FACE SHAPES

'Every human face approximates more or less to a type, the individual characteristics being worked out within definite limits set by heredity and environment; and men's faces, long or classic ovals, squared or rounded or sharp-featured, may easily enough be classified into a small or a large number of typical forms.'

From *The Human Face* by John Brophy.

The human head, at least as far as the artist is concerned, resembles an egg sitting narrow end down atop a cylinder. If the egg-shape is bisected by a horizontal line, it marks the head's equator, upon which stand the eyes. To the north reside the twin hedges of the eyebrows, the pale desert of the forehead, and, most distant of all, the forest of hair—or, in the case of those, like myself, who have been denuded by Time's scythe, the mosquitoes' landing strip. To the south, as might perhaps be expected, the landscape is more varied and interesting:

> Coming to kiss her lyps, (such grace I found,)
> Me seemd, I smelt a gardin of sweet flowres,
> That dainty odours from them threw around,
> For damzels fit to deck their lovely bowres.
> Her lips did smell lyke unto Gillyflowers;
> Her ruddy cheekes, lyke unto Roses red;
> Her snowy browes, like budded Bellamoures;
> Her lovely eyes, lyke Pincks but newly spred . . .

Or so poetized Edmund Spenser upon the lovely countenance of one Elizabeth, with whom he fell deeply in love, and to whom, after first suffering her rejection and indifference, he was finally married. He celebrated this happy event by composing his wonderful *Epithalamion*, in which he touches upon his wife's interior loveliness, mirroring that of her face:

> But if ye saw that which no eye can see,
> The inward beauty of her lively spright,
> Garnisht with heavenly guifts of high degree,
> Much more then would ye wonder at that sight,
> And stand astonisht lyke to those which red
> Medusaes mazeful hed.

But few heads, if any, have the perfect egg-like symmetry of the artist's imaginary model, and by no means all faces are oval in shape. Different skull types, fatty deposits, hair-lines and fleshy thickenings produce other geometries, which in themselves, where the face is concerned, form variations on the magic threesome of the circle, the square, and the triangle; and these, when upturned, form a fourth, the inverted triangle, balancing on one point, each corresponding to one of the four elements of Empedocles (see Figure 8).

The circle represents Water; the square, Earth; the upright triangle, Fire; and the inverted triangle, Air. These shapes correspond to the four ancient character types. The round-faced have a watery or phlegmatic temperament; the square-faced, an earthy or melancholic temperament; the upright triangle-faced, a fiery or choleric temperament; and the inverted triangle-faced, an airy or sanguine temperament.

But in the everyday world it is common to meet up with intermediate types, whose geometry has been somewhat modified. For exam-

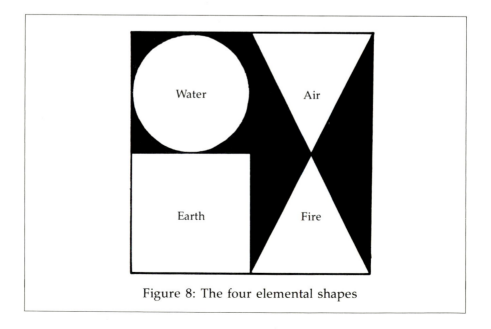

Figure 8: The four elemental shapes

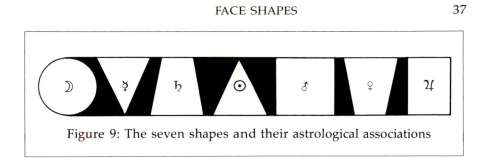

Figure 9: The seven shapes and their astrological associations

ple, a face with an equality of width may have sufficient height to form a rectangle; an upright triangle face that lacks its peak has the shape of a volcanic cone; and an inverted triangle face with a square jaw looks more like a bucket. These variations, together with the four basic shapes, give seven principal face shapes, and you should find your own face resembles one or other of them (see Figure 9).

Furthermore, these seven shapes can each be identified with one of the seven traditional planets of astrology, which are the Moon, Mercury, Venus, the Sun, Mars, Jupiter and Saturn. The circle symbolizes the Moon; the inverted triangle, Mercury; the volcano, Saturn; the upright triangle, the Sun; the square, Mars; the bucket, Venus; and the rectangle, Jupiter. In fact you may discover that your personality accords with one of the seven basic types described below:

THE ROUND FACE

This face shape is alternatively known as the Water or Moon face and is possessed by those with a phlegmatic temperament. If you have a round face you may also be fat and flabby, although such rotundity of person does not always accompany a round face. For example, Giacomo Soranzo wrote of Mary Tudor, 'She is of low stature, with a red and white complexion, and very thin; her eyes are white and large, and her hair reddish; her face is round, with a nose rather low and wide.' And her father, Henry VIII, was described as having 'a round face, so very beautiful that it would become a pretty woman, his throat being rather long and thick.'

The complexion of the round-faced tends towards paleness, which is indicative of poor circulation and a weak heart, and the eyes and lips and hair often appear to have been drained of colour. The skin is sensitive to sunlight, and injudicious sunbathing results in an unbecoming redness. The fine, weak hair is difficult to manage or style. The forehead is quite low, but is broad and rounded. The eyes are watery and staring, and rounded in form. The nose is short in length, often upturned and rather flat. A good example of a round face is shown in Figure 10.

Figure 10: The round or Moon face

If you have a round face you probably lack energy and are rather lazy, preferring to put off until tomorrow what should really be done today. Yet such prevarication is often a ploy to force others to do what you don't want to do, which can cause anger and resentment on their part. Indeed, you like being waited on and cossetted, as you have a dependent disposition, and you are fond of the comforts of life. As you find it hard to make decisions, you are a follower and not a leader. In fact you always take the line of least resistance. You lack self-confidence, which is why if you are going to make anything of your life you need plenty of support and encouragement. You enjoy country life and travel by boat. Hard work frightens you and you do your best to avoid it.

You have a rich dream world and plenty of imagination, so that you always have plenty of ideas about what you could be doing. Your forward progress is hampered not only by your laziness, but also by your changeable nature and by the ease with which you become bored. You are also the victim of your own imaginings, especially where your health is concerned: any ache or pain, no matter how innocuous, becomes magnified into the symptom of some dreadful and incurable disease. Yet despite these somewhat negative character traits, you are also good-humoured, easy-going, gentle and friendly, and you are always ready to help someone in need.

However, if you have a round face but also a long nose and power-ful eyes, such as we see in the face of Mayumi Hachiya (see Figure 19), then you have a more dynamic personality. Your brain is quick, your energy is greater, and you have a need to make an impression on the world.

THE SQUARE FACE

This shape of face is also known as the Earth or Mars face and it betokens a melancholic temperament. It is distinguished by its equality of width and by the fact that its width and height are approximately the same. Those with this face shape usually have a strong, muscular body and are of medium height. The complexion is ruddy, which reflects the good health and vitality of the type, although the redness of the white of the eyes is an unattractive feature. The eyes are large, dark and commanding, and the eyebrows are bushy. The broad forehead is not very high. The nose is wide, moderately long, and has a convex, or pugnacious, curvature. The mouth is usually large, yet the lips are thin and the teeth small. The square, strong chin looks as though it could take a hard punch. The small ears are set close to the head. An example of a square face is shown in Figure 11.

If you have a square face you are likely to be a tough, determined and aggressively energetic sort of person, with a quick temper and an unnerving tendency to shoot first and ask questions afterwards.

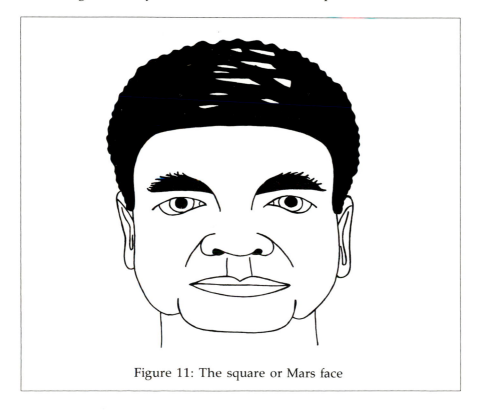

Figure 11: The square or Mars face

Those around you have to tread carefully, as you easily take offence, although you soon forgive and forget. You shout a lot and your voice is loud. You have a strong constitution and good health, which is why you are seldom ill. You like using your body, whether to do physical work or to play rough, body-contact games like rugby, as you are a doer rather than a thinker. You are impatient and impulsive, which is why you often do stupid things and get yourself into trouble. You like your own way and you're not afraid to thump the table with your fist to make a point. You resemble the round-faced person in your selfishness, although you are more direct and forceful in this respect.

Having a sociable nature, you enjoy company, particularly that of the opposite sex, yet your manners and tastes are somewhat crude. But while you are happy with your loved ones and friends, you wither like an unwatered plant when alone. In fact you hate to be by yourself, as you lack inner strength, and solitude can easily precipitate the black depressions—your melancholia—to which you are prone. In this respect you are like Samuel Johnson's 'old friend', Sober, by whom he means himself, who 'trembles at the thought' of being left to his own devices.

THE UPRIGHT TRIANGLE FACE

This face shape is also known as the Fire or Sun face and is symbolic of a choleric or angry temperament. It is distinguished by its wide jaw and by the narrow, often pointed, forehead. A person with this face has a physique much like that of the square-faced individual, with whom he or she has much in common. The eyes of this type are normally large, bright and striking, yet their pale colour and intensity of gaze can be unnerving, and they are crowded by the low-set eyebrows. The hair is plentiful and wavy, and is typically blond or fair in colour. It is very unusual for the male with this face shape to go bald. His beard also grows well, its luxuriance accentuating the width of the jaw and so giving its owner a bandit-like appearance. The large ears stand out from the sides of the head. The long nose, if it has not been broken in a fight, usually has a pugnacious outward curvature. Figure 12 illustrates this face shape.

If you have this type of face, which resembles a candle flame in outline, you will have had a difficult childhood, which is the key to your anger and to your desire to become a somebody. But while you possess drive, you lack patience to attain what you want through honest labour and so may be tempted to use underhand or even illegal methods. But you are lucky, and it is this, together with your persuasive tongue and aggressive manner, that can sometimes take you far. However, your loyalties are not strong and you have no

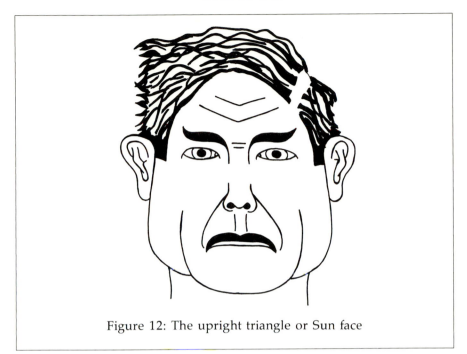

Figure 12: The upright triangle or Sun face

qualms about backing another horse if the going gets rough.

You can be charming and pleasant when it suits you, yet very nasty when you lose your self-control, which easily happens when you are frustrated or disobeyed. Indeed, your bad temper and violent disposition make you a danger to both yourself and others. You are also highly sexed, and you may become a stud or *femme fatale* if you have the looks and the opportunity, but a potential rapist (if you are a man) or a molester if you don't. You like to boast about how wonderful you are, but unfortunately your talents seldom match up to the claims you make for them.

THE TRUNCATED UPRIGHT TRIANGLE FACE

This face shape is a variant of the above, although it is met with far more commonly in everyday life. It is also known as the Volcano or Saturn face. The jaw is likewise wider than the forehead, yet the difference in width between the two is not so great, and the straight, yet short hair-line reflects an earthy or melancholic component of the otherwise choleric temperament. Those with this type of face are often quite tall and slim in build, with long thigh bones and prominent knees and knuckles. The face itself is bony, having sharp angles, outstanding cheekbones, hollow cheeks, and sunken eyes. The lack of facial softness is made more apparent by the white or

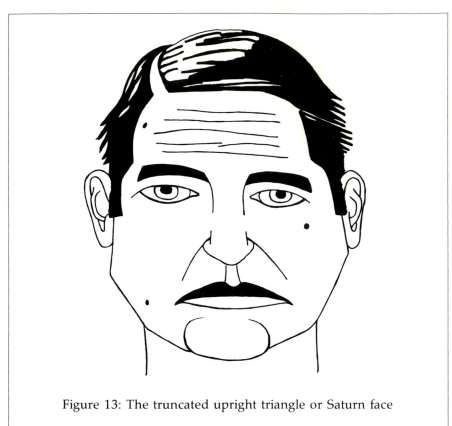

Figure 13: The truncated upright triangle or Saturn face

yellow skin and by the presence of moles and other blemishes. The forehead is high, but narrow, and usually bears many creases. The eyebrows are thick and bushy, and press down like a weight upon the dark eyes. The nose is large, often aquiline, and has long, narrow and rigid nostrils. The mouth is also large, its thin lips giving it a coarse and mirthless appearance. The thick growth of beard crowds the mouth unflatteringly, and when left unshaven hides the cheeklines and adds further breadth to the wide jaw. The skin is cold to the touch. An example of this face shape is shown in Figure 13.

If your face has this shape, then your early years were probably not very happy, which accounts, as it does with the former type, for your inner anger. Yet you have more self-control than the person with the upright triangle face shape, and you express your dislike or annoyance by means of barbed criticism, rather than by shouting or by throwing things. You have no great love for your fellow man and you prefer to spend your time alone with your thoughts. Yet you have strong opinions and you are not afraid of speaking your mind.

Your interests are both of a solitary nature and somewhat unusual, like fell walking and bird watching, and which get you outside. You enjoy pondering the deeper questions of life and you often have some interesting, even original, ideas. Yet you lack warmth and a desire to share, hence others tend to miss out on your wisdom. You are instinctively careful, cautious and conservative, especially in your handling of money, which is why you may become well-off but never rich. Although you have a strong sex drive, your innate shyness and awkwardness make it hard for you to find a mate, so that you are likely to feel frustrated and misunderstood. Indeed, there is a danger that your repressed energies may get channelled into some odd or even perverted activities.

THE INVERTED TRIANGLE FACE

This face shape is widest across the forehead and narrowest across the chin, and is thus the opposite of the previous two types. It is alternatively known as the Air or Mercury face and symbolizes a bright, cheerful or sanguine temperament. While those with such a face are not usually very tall, their bodies are lithe and well-proportioned. The facial features are typically regular and balanced, except for the mouth which may be either too small or too large. The skin is smooth and clear, the complexion olive. The large eyes may either be light in colour or dark, sometimes almost black. The nose has a thin bridge, yet often flares at its base to form large nostrils. The teeth are small and nicely shaped. Figure 14 shows an example of this face shape.

If you have this rather unusual type of face, with its wide forehead and pointed chin, then you are probably a nervous, fraught sort of person, who has great difficulty in relaxing and keeping still. In fact you may have been a hyperactive child. Your physical restlessness is matched by that of your brain, which is endlessly thinking and worrying, or absorbing facts. You like to know things, and the more information you learn the better, as knowledge gives you status and power. You prefer to work with your head rather than your hands, and you have a talent for teaching and organizing others. You love talking and arguing, and your quick wits and persuasive tongue not only enable you to influence your fellows in a general sense, but give you the ability to sell goods, mediate disputes, arrange meetings and functions, and suggest solutions to problems. In this respect you are a born politician. You are ambitious, but

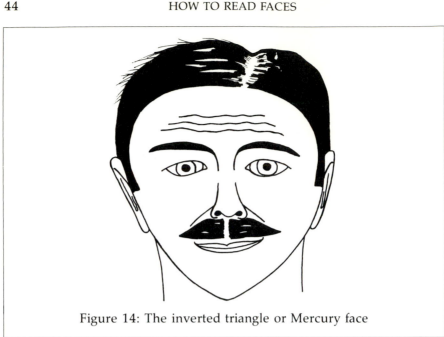

Figure 14: The inverted triangle or Mercury face

because you can be sly, underhand and exploitative, you may make powerful enemies that can stop you from reaching your goals. And while you enjoy meeting new people, you have few close friends; indeed, emotional closeness disturbs you.

THE AMPUTATED INVERTED TRIANGLE FACE

This is a commonly occurring face shape and is the one that comes closest to the oval face beloved of the artist. It is also known as the Bucket or Venus face. It is typically rather feminine in appearance, having as it does a certain roundness of form and softness of substance. The eyes are large and possess both long lashes and an attractive sparkle. The straight nose has nostrils which enlarge and contract like a horse's at moments of excitement. The red, shapely lips border a large mouth and give the female a sexy look. The skin is soft, clear and radiant, and the cheeks have a rosy hue. The thick hair grows quickly and looks at its best when it is long. The strongly fashioned jaw forms the most masculine part of the face. An example of this face type is shown in Figure 15.

If your face has this shape you are warm and affectionate, with an outgoing, generally upbeat personality. You like other people and enjoy their company, and always try to think the best of them. Such attitudes help you to both gain friends and have an active and varied

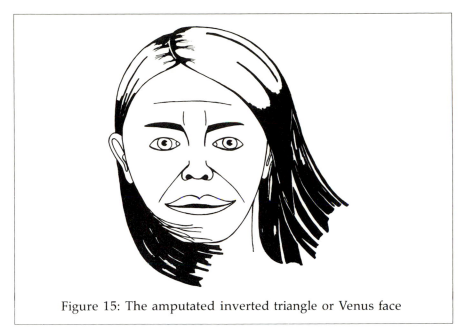

Figure 15: The amputated inverted triangle or Venus face

social life. You seldom get depressed and when you do your blue moods thankfully don't last for long. You have wide interests, although you're more fond of the arts than anything else. You particularly like singing, dancing and the theatre. Romance is important to you and you will probably marry young, as you like the idea of having a home, a spouse, and children. Your wit is ready, but it is gentle and kind. Yet because you are too trusting, you easily fall victim to those who could take advantage of you. If you have poor facial features, you may be lethargic and rather coarse; you will certainly be fascinated by the seamy side of life.

THE RECTANGULAR FACE

This face is characterized by its length, which is greater than its width, and by its uniformity of breadth, wherein it resembles the square face. It is also known as the Tree Bole or Jupiter face. It is typically possessed by those who are either born to, or rise to, a high position in life. Queen Elizabeth I had a face that was 'oblong, fair, and wrinkled' (as reported in her 65th year), and so did the philosopher Thomas Hobbes.

In essence it is a dignified and pleasant face. The forehead is high and broad, rising steeply above the arched eyebrows and gaining height, at least in the man, from the receding hair-line. One or more well-marked horizontal creases are usually present upon it. The eyes

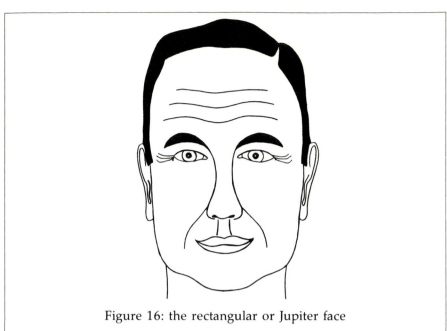

Figure 16: the rectangular or Jupiter face

are large, clear and bright, and focus on the world with a look of interest. Wrinkles decorate their corners, adding dignity and sagacity to the expression. The nose is of either the Greek or Roman type, and is long, broad and prominent. The large-lobed ears are set close to the head. The medium-sized mouth, with its distinct, yet not full, lips, does not detract from the firmness of the chin. The skin is smooth and fine, its paleness brightened by touches of red on the cheeks.

You are fortunate if you possess this shape of face, because it symbolizes an honest, upstanding character and an often remarkable destiny. Indeed, you have all the warmth and optimism of the previous type, without its attendant weaknesses. You are blessed with great energy, strong ideals, and an unshakeable fixity of purpose. You not only find it easy to make friends, but also soon gain both their love and respect. You believe in honest dealing and the rule of law, and you stick up both for your own rights and those of others. You are well suited to leadership, not only because you want the top job, but because you know how to treat those under you, whom you direct by example, not exhortation.

You have quite strong religious beliefs, which while normally a positive influence in your life, can become warped in the wrong circumstances, so causing you to imagine that you've been specially chosen by God. Such an unfortunate development can turn your mirth into malice, your confidence into arrogance, and, worst of all, your benevolence into tyranny.

Chapter Four
DATING THE FACE

'There was something in his physiognomy which caught Harley's notice: indeed, physiognomy was one of Harley's foibles, for which he had been often rebuked by his aunt in the country, who used to tell him that when he had come to her years and experience he would know that all's not gold that glisters.'

From *The Man of Feeling* by Henry Mackenzie.

The shape of your face can only serve as a general guide to your character and fate. Much more detail is shown by your features, which can in fact be used to foretell the major events of your life. How such events are dated is the subject of this chapter. I appreciate that the reader may be sceptical that either past or future happenings can be divined from the face, but I ask you to bear with me and to examine the evidence presented with a dispassionate mind.

We are indebted to the Chinese for the system of facial dating outlined here. I have, however, made one small change to their method. In China it is usual to regard a child as being one year old at birth, whereas we in the West date a child's age from its birth. Hence I have retrograded the age points familiar to the Chinese physiognomist by one year, so as to bring them into line with our system of ageing.

If an imaginary line is drawn down the centre of a face, so dividing it into two halves, 13 important age positions are found to lie along it (see Figure 17). These in fact bestride the line, so to speak, to take in an area of flesh up to half an inch in width, depending on the position, on either side of the line. Each is evaluated depending on its colour and condition and by the shape and quality of the facial part it occupies. Dry or greasy skin, blackheads and whiteheads, moles, and

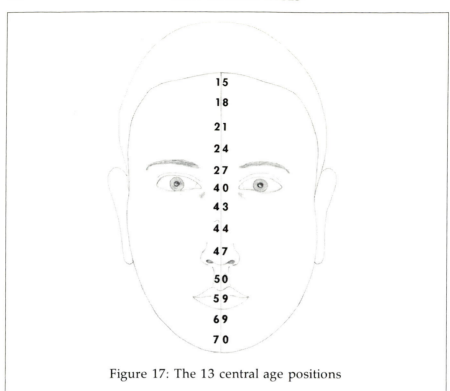

Figure 17: The 13 central age positions

imperfections caused by accident or disease, are all considered to detract from the meaning of the position where they occur.

Four positions—representing ages 15, 18, 21, and 24—lie on the forehead. One, known as Yin T'ang, or the 'Seat of the Seal', representing age 27, lies between the eyebrows. Another four—signifying ages 40, 43, 44, and 47—are placed on the nose. One position, that of age 50, is identified with the philtrum, or groove, joining the nose with the upper lip. One—representing age 59—corresponds to the central portion of the upper and lower lips, and two—representing ages 69 and 70—are situated on the chin.

From this it can be seen that the top of the forehead corresponds to the youngest of these ages and that as we proceed down the face the lower areas relate to increasingly older ages. The ears in fact symbolize the earliest years of life, from birth to age 13, and the other age positions are represented by those facial features, like the eyebrows, that run across the face at right angles to the perpendicular central line.

The interpretation of these 13 primary positions is made somewhat difficult by the fact that certain of them refer to one or other of your relatives as well as to yourself. And where you are concerned, they both indicate aspects of your character and presage events in your life at the age they signify. And they can also, by changing colour for example, forewarn of coming problems in your life irrespective of what age you are. Hence they require evaluating with caution.

POSITION 15

This is called T'ien Chun by the Chinese; it is the highest position of the mid-line and its upper border is typically formed by the hair-line. It primarily signifies your father and your relationship with him. Ideally, the site should be gently rounded and the skin smooth, unblemished and radiantly pink in colour. If so, it suggests that your father is fortunate in matters of health and career, and that your relationship with him was and is good. However, should the position show negative features—by being indented, for instance, or by having a poor skin colour or quality—then your childhood will not have been so happy with regard to your father and his own fortune will not have been as blessed.

The hair-line sometimes projects downwards into position 15 to form a point, such as can be seen in the drawing of the film star

Figure 18: Robert Taylor

Robert Taylor (see Figure 18). If your hair-line shows this feature, it reveals that you have both artistic talents and an artistic temperament. It also indicates that your father will die before your mother. When this position takes on a dark colour, especially if it persists, it is a negative sign, suggesting ill luck.

POSITION 18

This forehead area, which bears the Chinese name T'ien T'ing, signifies the qualities that you inherited from your mother, your relationship with her, and your mother's own fortune. If the site is gently rounded, unblemished, and has a clear, bright colouring, it betokens good luck in all these respects. Indeed, if both this position and position 15 above it have such characteristics, then your relations with both of your parents were and are satisfactory, as were the guidelines for living that you received from them. Conversely, if both positions are less ideally formed—by being indented or by having a poor complexion, for example—they reveal a less happy situation between you and your parents.

If this position has a grey or dark colouration, or is dull and lacking in life, it is a negative character sign, suggesting that you tend to be disbelieved, even when you are telling the truth. In this respect you are rather like the foolish shepherd boy in the fable by Aesop who cried 'Wolf!' as a joke once too often, and found to his consternation that when some wolves actually did appear, nobody paid him any attention and he lost all his sheep. Hence you would be well-advised to avoid spinning tales, exaggerating or prevaricating, so as to build up other people's confidence in you. In this way you'll be able to limit any damage that might otherwise be done to you.

When any unusual change of colour occurs in this position—and bluish, greenish and yellowish-red colorations are the worst—it presages imminent bad luck. So don't take any unnecessary risks when such a colour change happens!

POSITION 21

The ancient Chinese name for this area is Ssu Kung, although because it relates to career success, it is alternatively known as Kuan Lu Kung or the 'Career Palace'. In fact this position, along with position 18 above and position 24 below, together form an area called the 'Seat of Honours'. A fortunate Seat of Honours is always found on the foreheads of those who become famous or honoured, whereas a flawed one reveals that such success will elude its owner.

Ideally, position 21 should be gently rounded, have a radiant sheen, and be otherwise unblemished. So formed, it not only indicates that your 21st year was, is or will be favourable for you, but that your career prospects in general are very good. You will be helped to get ahead by those interested in your welfare, and you will be blessed in life by having kind and thoughtful friends.

If the colour of this position changes to grey or becomes dark, or if it takes on a dull appearance, it reveals that your career is under threat and that you can expect some bad luck. But as being forewarned is forearmed, you can use such a negative colour change to prepare yourself for the worst and to perhaps take damage-limiting countermeasures.

POSITION 24

As Figure 17 shows, this position, which the Chinese call Chung Cheng, lies immediately above the gap between the eyebrows; it forms the basal third of the Seat of Honours. It presages early success and general good fortune if it is gently rounded, clear of dull moles, spots and other blemishes, and has a radiant colour.

Should position 24 be hollow or indented and dark in colour, it is one sign of a low intellect, which in itself is detrimental to the gaining of success in life. However, if such a negative sign is partnered by other facial features indicative of high intelligence, it means that for psychological or other reasons the inherited IQ is not being fully utilized.

When this position bears one or more black moles or a scar, or has skin defects like spots, it betokens impatience and irritability, and in turn friction with others. Moles, being permanent, reveal innate tendencies of this type; scars suggest an acquired testiness; and spots, etc., betray a temporary lack of cool.

Figure 19 is a drawing of the North Korean terrorist Kim Hyon-hui, who is better known by her assumed Japanese name of Mayumi Hachiya. On 12 November 1987, after an eight-year period of training organized for her by Kim Jong-il, the son of North Korea's leader, and at his behest, she planted a bomb aboard Korean Air Flight 858, which was travelling from Baghdad to Seoul. She and her partner, Kim Sung-il, left the plane at Abudhabi. The bomb exploded when the plane was flying over the Andaman Sea, west of Burma. All 115 passengers and crew were killed.

Mayumi Hachiya is therefore a mass-murderess. But she is not a born criminal like Junzo Okudairo—she had in fact been a child actress—and was only chosen to become a terrorist because both her parents were trusted members of the Communist Korean Workers'

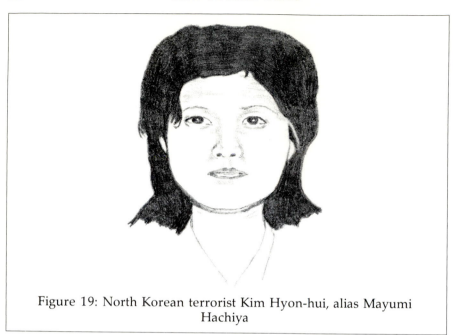

Figure 19: North Korean terrorist Kim Hyon-hui, alias Mayumi
Hachiya

Party. This is why her face does not show the obvious asymmetry of
Okudairo's or even most of the features which Lombroso identified
with the criminal face. She does, of course, have thick, dark hair, yet
this is not unusual in an Oriental. Indeed, the only apparent indicator
of inherent criminality is the size of her face—it is half as wide again
as her neck—while its round or Moon shape suggests, as we have
already noted, a dependent and malleable personality, which can be
moulded into a fighting machine by an evil Svengali.

But what is interesting about her face where position 24 is concerned, is the projecting bony outgrowth which crosses her lower
forehead from the top of one eyebrow to the other, so passing
through position 24 and raising it to an unnatural prominence. Such
an elevation of the bottom portion of the Seat of Honours reveals that
she will achieve wide notoriety, not fame or fortune, in her mid-
twenties. And so she did. Mayumi Hachiya was 25 years old when
she planted that fateful bomb, and she now faces a life sentence—as
well as the risk of assassination—in a South Korean gaol.

FOREHEAD CREASES

Forehead creases that obliquely cross one or other of the afore-men-
tioned positions are negative in meaning and thus damaging in some

degree to those qualities or aspects of life signified by the position.

However, horizontal or transverse forehead creases are generally positive in meaning, unless they are broken or become frayed on the position that they cross. When this happens they rob the position of much of its symbolic good fortune. The interpretation of horizontal forehead creases is further considered in Chapter 7.

Sometimes one or more vertical creases rise from either the top of the nose or from the space between the eyebrows. These important lines must now be discussed. When a single crease rises through positions 24 and 21, or perhaps even higher (see Figure 20), it signifies the concentration of the mind on career goals and personal advancement, and is thus the mark of the person who is selfish, single-minded and ambitious.

It is not therefore surprising to find that those who attain a high position in life through their own efforts often have a single vertical forehead crease. Such people tend to make powerful enemies, which is why the single crease is called the 'Suspended Needle' by the Chinese, who picture it as a sort of sword of Damocles, representing those dangers that hover over them and which are likely to do them mischief when the time is right. And because those with a single crease are egotistical and self-centred, its presence usually indicates that their personal relationships are fraught and unsatisfying. But it should be remembered that there may be other features in the face which symbolize characteristics that can modify the intensity of those indicated by the single vertical crease. When these are not present the person concerned may suffer a premature and unnatural, or even a violent, death.

It is much more common to find two parallel creases rising vertically from the inner ends of the eyebrows. These signify a more balanced and less dogmatic and selfish character, which means that their

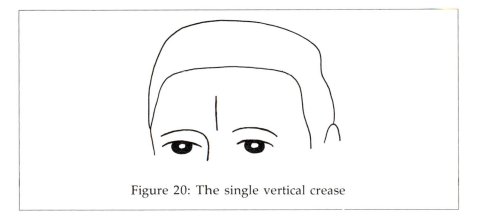

Figure 20: The single vertical crease

Figure 21: Brigitte Bardot

owner can see both sides of an argument and thus pays attention to the other fellow's point of view. Those with such creases—as, for example, the ex-film star Brigitte Bardot (see Figure 21)—may indeed rise to a prominent position in life, but they will keep their friends and be treated with respect.

However, if the two vertical creases slope towards one another (see Figure 22), as if they wished to merge and form one line, then this naturally indicates egocentric tendencies, which will create problems for the person concerned, particularly in the area of personal relationships.

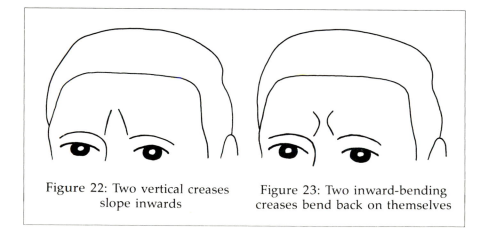

Figure 22: Two vertical creases slope inwards

Figure 23: Two inward-bending creases bend back on themselves

If the two creases slope inwards but then bend back upon themselves (see Figure 23), they reveal an egocentric tendency but at the same time a lack of guts in making use of it. Hence the person is uncertain of himself, wanting on the one hand to go in and make a killing, but hanging back on the other for fear of losing support and being rejected. This type is therefore lost in a psychological no man's land, pleasing nobody, not even himself. Thus it is difficult for such a person to reach a high position or indeed to achieve much to be proud of.

When the two vertical creases meander like rivers (see Figure 24), they symbolize great inner uncertainty and vacillation. Their owner will have difficulty in establishing himself in a career and may also face personal danger in later life.

It is a fortunate sign when three vertical creases rise into the Seat of Honours (see Figure 25). Such a marking signifies early success in life and the accompanying attainment of some celebrity. This also holds true if the two outer lines slope outwards, so forming a trident

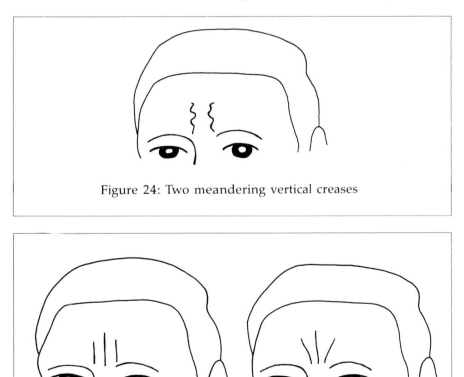

Figure 24: Two meandering vertical creases

Figure 25: Three vertical creases   Figure 26: Three creases form
a trident

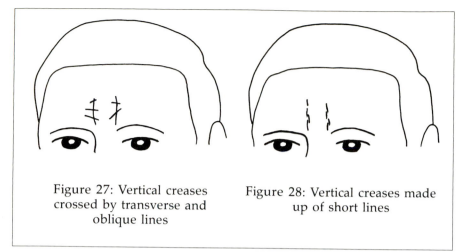

Figure 27: Vertical creases
crossed by transverse and
oblique lines

Figure 28: Vertical creases made
up of short lines

(see Figure 26), but not if they slope inwards, when they represent
selfishness and also an anxious disposition.

It is not favourable when the vertical creases are crossed by short
transverse or oblique lines (see Figure 27), especially if these are
deeply cut, as they are evidence of a tense, irritable nature, which
brings problems for the person concerned in his or her relationships.
Hence those having such cross lines are frequently unhappy and
dissatisfied.

When a single vertical crease is crossed by such lines it forms a
very unfortunate configuration, as it represents a strongly egocentric
person fighting against difficulties which he has largely brought
upon his own head, thereby producing an explosive inner cocktail of
anger, guilt and frustration. Such a person needs handling with care.

The vertical creases sometimes consist of a series of short lines
which give them an indistinct appearance (see Figure 28). This
formation robs them of their symbolic potency and force, hence
those with such lines will find that their efforts to establish
themselves are frustrated and thus personally disappointing in their
twenties. Yet if the other facial features are good, lost progress can be
made up later in life.

However, it is a very negative sign when three vertical creases are
either broken or wandering in form, or both (see Figure 29), as this is
symbolic of both mental impairment and a criminal tendency.

The presence of four or more vertical creases rising above the nose
is also a negative indication, no matter how well marked they are (see
Figure 30). Such a feature signifies a restless, shiftless person, the
drifter who prefers to live a wandering life on the outskirts of society
and who lacks motivating ambitions. He or she often has a drink or
drug problem.

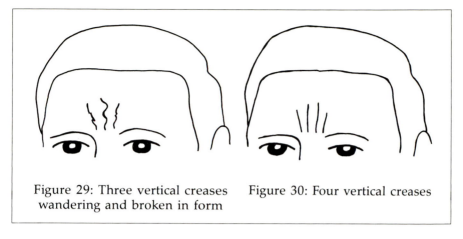

Figure 29: Three vertical creases wandering and broken in form

Figure 30: Four vertical creases

POSITION 27

This area lies between the eyebrows and is known to the Chinese as Yin T'ang or the 'Seat of the Seal'. It is sometimes also called the 'Life Region'. Together with position 40, it forms the most important part of the face, as they both reflect career success and longevity.

Position 27 should ideally be firm, gently rounded, broad and

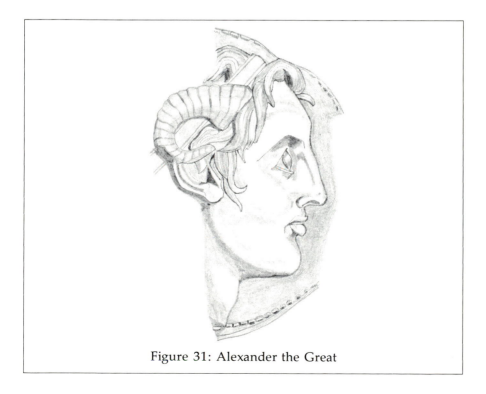

Figure 31: Alexander the Great

unblemished. If so, it symbolizes a successful career which will begin by or at age 27 and a measure of fame. And if the lower facial features are supporting, such career success will continue for many years.

Yet if the position is negatively formed, by being indented, for example, or if it bears one or more dull, dark moles, then little or no success can be anticipated during the early years of the career. Indeed, there is likely to be unhappiness and poor health.

When position 27 is moderately outstanding, it signifies a sharp and incisive mind and also great energy and determination. These are the qualities possessed by a born leader, which is why we find such an enlargement affecting both positions 24 and 27 on the head of Alexander the Great (see Figure 31). We can be reasonably sure that this is an accurate profile of the Macedonian conqueror, as the coin it graces was struck by his general, Lysimachus.

A broad position 27, which is produced by a wide gap between the eyebrows, is normally a positive indication, particularly for women, as it can presage wealth and fame. Many successful film stars, for instance, had or have such a broad space between their eyebrows. But when position 27 is wide and is accompanied by thin eyebrows, its meaning is less positive, for it also signifies an early death. We find this combination in the face of Jean Harlow (see Figure 32), who died of uremic poisoning at the age of 26.

Miss Harlow's irises, notwithstanding the fact that her head is bent downwards somewhat, are also positioned too high, which has the

Figure 32: Jean Harlow died trag-
ically young   Figure 33: Writer Roald Dahl

effect of making the whites of her eyes appear beneath them. This condition, as was mentioned earlier, is known as sanpaku and symbolizes a disturbed inner state. It is also one sign of a premature death. Her forehead lacks horizontal creases, which is indicative of a rather vacuous mind, while her hair-line is uneven, a feature that signifies a troubled childhood and which in turn suggests a disturbed adult—an analysis that is borne out by the floating irises.

Position 27 is occasionally crossed by one or more transverse creases. Such a crease is visible in the face of the writer Roald Dahl (see Figure 33); a second passes across the upper portion of position 40. These are the mark of an authoritarian personality, one who likes his or her own way and who expects others to mould themselves to his needs.

Colour changes affecting position 27 must always be taken seriously, as they are symptomatic of a developing disease condition. A blue colouration, for example, is one indicator of disordered kidneys, while a reddish colour is linked with heart abnormalities. Similarly, a darkening of the area warns of stomach ailments, such as a peptic ulcer. When the position bears a dull, dark mole it presages the development of a chronic disease like diabetes, at either age 27 or a little later in life.

The growth of hair on position 27 is not a positive sign, especially when the eyebrows grow across it to form a continuous line. The eyebrows symbolize a person's emotional type and also his or her relations with other people, hence such united eyebrows betoken controlled emotions, a lack of sympathy, and thus the capacity to run roughshod over the feelings of one's fellows.

POSITION 40

This position comprises the bridge of the nose lying between the eyes. Its Chinese name is Shan Ken or the 'Roots of the Mountain', the mountain in question presumably being the nose itself. It rivals the above-lying position 27 in importance, notably because it can presage premature death.

The elevation and width of position 40 can vary greatly from person to person. When the bridge of the nose forms a continuous line with the forehead, thereby creating the classic Greek nose, which is seen in the profile of Alexander the Great (see Figure 31), position 40 is high—indeed, it seldom ever exceeds this height—while on the other hand it may be so sunken that the bridge of the nose all but vanishes between the eyes. And likewise it may be very narrow at one extreme or have a breadth resembling the flat side of a plank at the other.

Western face readers traditionally regard a high position 40 as a negative feature, which symbolizes a foppish nature and hence a lover of luxury, the artistic dilettante. This, however, is nonsense. The person with a high position 40, always providing that the nose at this point is not too narrow, is made of sterner stuff, possessed as he or she is of great energy, which can be used either constructively or destructively—how else did Alexander the Great conquer half the world? Indeed a high position 40 is typically found in the faces of those who attain a position of some standing in the world by the time they are 40. But because we cannot predict fame from one feature alone, a high position 40 can only be regarded as an indicator of special achievement.

As the elevation of position 40 sinks, so also does both the individual's energy level and his or her ability to utilize that energy purposefully. Because the height of this area is created by the underlying bone, unlike the lower nose which is largely underlain by cartilage, and as bone is a tissue representative of force and resolve, then a lessening of bone matter reveals a diminution of these qualities. This explains why those with a very low or flat position 40, which is, incidentally, a nasal feature found in apes and monkeys, seldom if ever advance themselves in life. And because body energy ultimately generates resistance to disease, a low position 40 signifies a weaker state of health, which may itself result in a shorter life.

A high position 40 is possessed by those who often have problems with close relationships, due to their autocratic and high-handed manner. This type tends therefore to have an unhappy marriage and to be at odds with other family members. A lower position 40 is suggestive of a more easy-going and less egocentric nature, which is indicative of happier relationships, although if the area is too low, to the extent of becoming almost flat, then the person concerned is dominated by his family and friends. When the base of position 27

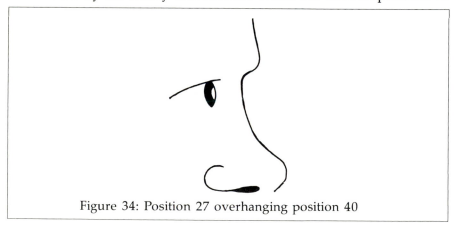

Figure 34: Position 27 overhanging position 40

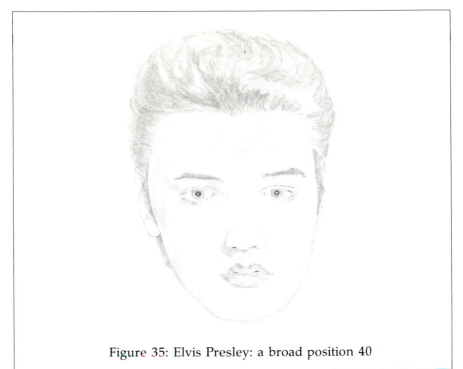

Figure 35: Elvis Presley: a broad position 40

overhangs this area (see Figure 34) it acts as a barrier to the free flow of energy between the two regions; this in turn symbolizes tiredness, a lack of resolve and indifferent health.

The width of position 40 is likewise of great importance. Some breadth is a positive sign as it symbolizes constancy and tenacity, or perseverance. Yet when the position is broad but low in elevation, such perseverance becomes stubbornness, which is often counter-productive in terms of getting ahead in life. Conversely, a narrow position 40 is indicative of poor concentration and lack of staying power, which can hinder, if not prevent, forward progress.

But when position 40 is so broad that it appears to fill, or almost fill, the space between the eyes, it acquires a sinister meaning by presaging a premature death—one that takes place by age 42 and which results from an accident, or from suicide or crime. We find such an unfortunate width of position 40 in the face of Elvis Presley, who died from a drug-induced heart attack, aged 42 (see Figure 35). In fact a glance at almost any newspaper photograph of someone who has died prematurely in strange circumstances will reveal this feature.

A mole on position 40 represents a lengthy period spent away from one's native land and can therefore presage emigration. The colour and shape of the mole (or moles) reveals how fortunate such a move will be. The luckiest moles are red or black in colour with a radiant sheen, and are round in shape. Grey or dark moles, especially if they are dull in appearance, or misshapen, or large in size, are unlucky and bode ill for such an adventure, which will thus be an unhappy and retrograde step. But no prediction should be made from the mole alone; it must be judged along with the other facial features, which may, for example, detract from the meaning of a fortunate mole, or enhance that of an unlucky mole.

A grey or dark tinge to the skin of position 40 is a sign of both poor vitality and of an incipient stomach or digestive disorder. A blue or red coloration of the area has the same meaning as that described for position 27. A crease or creases running transversely across position 40 signify a mid-life surgical operation.

POSITIONS 43, 44 AND 47

These all lie along the bridge of the nose and because they contribute to the overall nose shape, they will be considered in detail in Chapter 10. However, each is supported by a different tissue. Position 43, called Nien Shang by the Chinese, has a foundation of bone; position 44, whose Oriental name is Shou Shang, is cartilaginous; and position 47, named Chun T'ou, forms the nose tip and is constructed from muscle and fat. The years they represent are part of the prime mid-life period. Hence if each is firm, smooth, unblemished, and has a good colour, they reveal that your middle years will be healthy and happy, as they will be for your spouse and family at this time of your life.

A poor complexion—i.e. dryness or greasiness, spots, blackheads, etc.—blemishes like obliquely marked creases, dull moles or warts, or any skin discoloration affecting these positions are all suggestive of reduced vitality and poor health during the middle years, of problems with your spouse, and of sickness in the family. Sexual difficulties are also likely at this time if the skin quality is poor. The nose bridge should neither be too narrow, when it indicates narrowness of views, undue caution, and stinginess, nor too broad, which is suggestive of a lack of focus, financial improvidence, and a dissolute life-style.

POSITION 50

The Chinese refer to this position as Jen Chung or the 'Middle Man', and it constitutes the philtrum or groove which connects the nose with the centre of the upper lip. It is a very important part of the face, not only because it reveals your ability to have children, but also because it can help show how long you are going to live.

The best philtrum is long, straight, broad and deep, with distinct sides that create a channel along which life's energies can symbolically flow from the nose to the lips. Such a conduit is representative of fertility, and of a long life and good fortune, as well as revealing that your 50s will get off to a good start.

However, it is rare to come across such a well-made philtrum, for the simple reason that few people are so blessed by fortune. Indeed, it is usual for the philtrum to be shallower, which allows the life energies to be dissipated by their overflowing of the banks. Shallowness therefore represents a moderation of the fortunate happenings outlined above, which will be scanty indeed if the philtrum is very shallow, or completely absent if it is flat.

When the philtrum has the appearance of a river delta, so that it is wider at the bottom than at the top (see Figure 36), it indicates that you are fertile and are likely to have several children—if you so choose.

But when the opposite is the case, and the philtrum is wider at the top than at the bottom, so causing a restriction of the energy flow, then your fertility is low and you are thus unlikely to have many, if any, children (see Figure 37). A shallow philtrum will obviously make the situation worse. Such a shape is also detrimental to your general fortune, as it signifies frustrations and difficulties in your career and personal life, notably at age 50 and thereafter. Hence unless your lower face shows some moderating features, which indicate better luck, then you must expect your life to become increasingly problematic as you grow older.

The philtrum is sometimes broadest at its mid-point, which gives it more the appearance of a lake than a channel, wherein the energy stands rather than flows (see Figure 38). This in turn represents a stagnation in your fortunes in middle age, which may be brought about by illness, depression, or by events suddenly going against

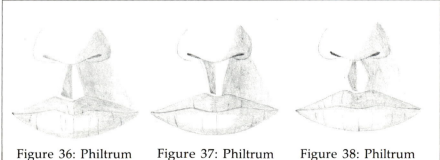

Figure 36: Philtrum   Figure 37: Philtrum   Figure 38: Philtrum
widest at its base   widest as its top   widest at its middle

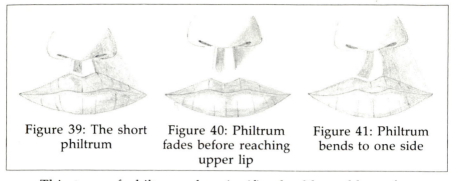

Figure 39: The short philtrum   Figure 40: Philtrum fades before reaching upper lip   Figure 41: Philtrum bends to one side

you. This type of philtrum also signifies health problems for your children.

If your philtrum fades and disappears before it reaches your upper lip, or if it is very short due to the fact that your upper lip lies close to your nose (see Figure 39), then your life will not be longer than 50 years. A short philtrum of the second type can be seen in the coin profile of Alexander the Great (see Figure 31), who died at age 32.

However, if your philtrum is long but falters and fades just before it reaches your upper lip (see Figure 40), then your death will occur later, although your declining years will be troubled by financial worries and by disagreements with your children, who may abandon you.

A philtrum that bends either to the right or to the left detracts from the balance of the face and is therefore a negative sign (see Figure 41). It augurs childlessness and also a loss of direction in mid-life. Should a bent philtrum form part of a general asymmetry of the lower part of your face, the two together signify that your later years will be blighted by ill-health, personal worries and financial hardship.

It is unfavourable for the philtrum to be crossed by one or more crease lines (see Figure 42a), which not only show that childlessness is likely, but that outside problems will crop up to spoil your middle years. But when a single line runs down the centre of the philtrum, it

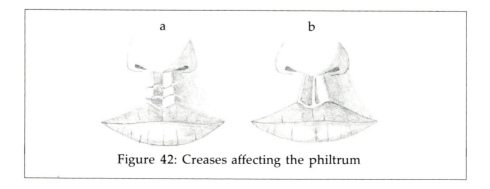

a   b

Figure 42: Creases affecting the philtrum

shows that a child or children will be conceived late in life—at about age 40 if you are a woman, or older if you are a man. (see Figure 42b).

Where men are concerned, it is considered fortunate if the hair of your moustache grows in the philtrum, always providing that the other features of your moustache and beard are good, as this indicates that you enjoy friendly relations with your fellows and have few, if any, enemies. But if your philtrum is devoid of hair, so that your moustache, when grown, appears to be parted down the middle, it signifies that you will upset others in some way and thereby gain enemies. Your later life will therefore suffer somewhat as a result.

POSITION 59

From an academic standpoint this position occupies the centre of the lips, but it can really be taken to include the lips as a whole. Hence we shall consider it fully in Chapter 11, which is devoted to the mouth and lips. The Chinese name for position 59 is Shui Hsing, and they consider it to be potentially the most beautiful of the face. In general, lips that are thin, dry and pale are symbolic of cruelty, vindictiveness and a lack of passion, whereas lips that are plumper, moister and redder betoken a warmer and more loving disposition, and therefore a happier life.

POSITION 69

This position, which the Chinese call Ch'eng Chiang, occupies the upper half of the chin beneath the lips. When the jaw is strongly formed, it is vertical or nearly so; but with a weaker jaw it slopes inwards, and the greater the slope, the greater the physical weakness associated with it. But while this position is linked with the 69th year of your age, it also relates to liquids and to the dangers that might be posed by them throughout your life. For example, when it takes on a dull, dark hue you should not swim or travel by boat, as your life will be in danger if you do. And similarly, if the area develops a dull, red coloration, it warns that you may drink something harmful if you're not careful, or that you may suffer from a stomach upset, or even that you may become the victim of a violent attack. Such colour changes are obviously of greater significance if you are 69 years old, as they forewarn of your imminent death.

A man should be able to grow hair on position 69. If so, he is largely immune from the dangers of drowning and poisoning, although his other facial features must be evaluated before such a positive pronouncement can be made. Lack of hair growth here is a negative sign because it presages almost constant danger from liquids, which includes those that are drunk for refreshment.

POSITION 70

This is the lowest of the 13 mid-line facial positions and is known to the Chinese as Ti Ko. Ideally, the region should be slightly uptilted, firm and strong in appearance, and the chin rounded. When so formed, it is the mark of a happy and contented old age. Yet position 70 cannot be so positively interpreted in a man if it lacks the ability to grow hair. Hence a weakly bearded or bald position 70, even though it is strongly formed, augurs a troubled and unhappy old age.

A pointed chin is never a favourable feature, as it not only indicates that its owner must struggle against adversity, but that his or her old age will be poverty-stricken and friendless. A pointed chin that bends to one side belongs to the person who never forgets a wrong and who always gets even, no matter how long it takes. Such an individual is disloyal and unkind, which is why he or she is miserable and unhappy, particularly in old age.

The ancient seers said that when position 70 develops a radiant red coloration, it signifies the coming of a happy event or a stroke of good luck. Yet when it turns a dull red it warns of danger from fire.

The mid-line upon which these 13 positions are arranged should ideally be straight and exactly vertical. When it is, it brings out the best in them, so that if the positions are well-formed and of good colour, etc., the qualities of character and the life events associated with them will find their most positive expression. In fact a straight mid-line reduces the intensity of those negative characteristics and life events which are suggested by badly formed or discoloured positions, or which bear unlucky moles or other blemishes.

And likewise, when the mid-line is not straight or vertical, it detracts from whatever good qualities the positions have with regard to form, colour and radiance. It is quite common, for example, to come across people whose lower jaw does not sit properly against their upper jaw, with the result that it is twisted to one side or the other. This bends the lower mid-line and so negatively affects those positions which relate to their middle age and old age, which will therefore be less happy and healthy than they would like. If such a bend affects positions that are themselves defective in some way, then only the worst can be predicted for the person concerned.

Figure 43 shows both the 13 central positions and the relationship of the other ages to the different parts of the face. From this you can see that the first 13 years of life are linked with the ears, the initial 6

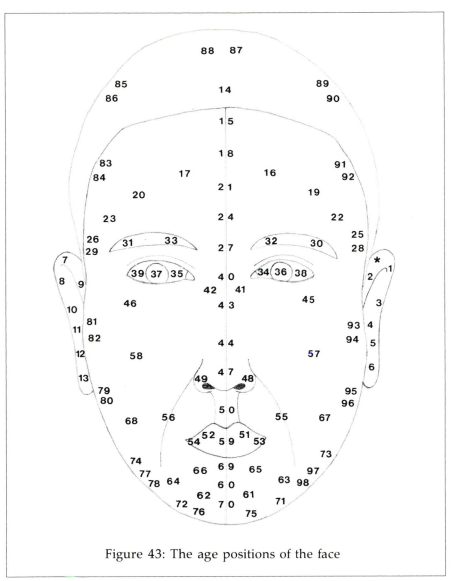

Figure 43: The age positions of the face

to the left ear and the next 7 to the right ear. The remaining teenage years are associated with the middle and upper forehead. The 20s are likewise indicated by the middle forehead and also by the temples; the 30s by the eyebrows and eyes; the 40s by the nose and cheek-bones; the 50s by the philtrum, mouth, cheeklines and cheeks; the 60s and 70s by the chin and its undersurface; the 80s by the right side of the face and head, etc.; and the 90s by the left side of the face and head. We shall refer to them all in those chapters dealing with the individual facial parts.

Chapter Five
PARTS AND
PROPORTIONS

'In passing, we will express an opinion that Nature never writes a bad hand. Her writing, as may be read in the human countenance, is invariably legible, if we come at all trained to the art of reading it.'

From *Household Words.*

The face, when viewed from the front, can be divided into three areas or zones, each of which relates to specific facets of our character and, as we have already noted, to certain years in our lives. The three zones are illustrated in Figure 44.

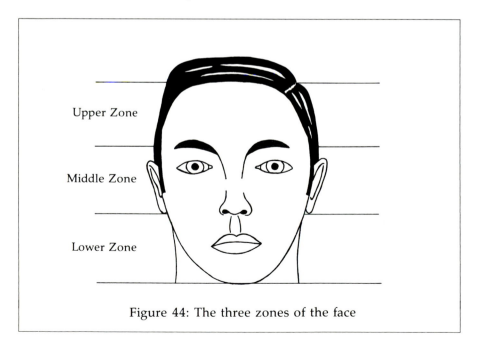

Upper Zone

Middle Zone

Lower Zone

Figure 44: The three zones of the face

The highest or Upper Zone is formed by the forehead and extends downwards from the hair-line to the eyebrows. The Chinese call it the Heavenly Area. The Middle Zone, or Human Area, encompassing the eyes, nose and cheeks, extends downwards from the eyebrows to the bottom of the nose; while the Lower Zone, or Earth Area, which includes the mouth and the chin, forms that portion of the face lying beneath the nose.

The Upper Zone signifies our intellectual capacity, the Middle Zone our adaptability, and the Lower Zone our inherent energy or drive. These three primary qualities of character, viz. intelligence, adaptability, and energy, largely determine how well we relate to others and to the world, and thus how successfully we proceed through life. The ability to adapt, by which we express our intellect and energy, is perhaps the most important of the three, although without brain power we may set our sights too low, and with insufficient energy we may give up too easily and thus fail in our endeavours.

Ideally, therefore, we need an approximately equal measure of these three qualities, and when such a balance exists it is revealed in the face by an equal development of the three zones and by the straightness of the mid-line. Yet perfect balance is only seen in the faces of exceptional people, hence we should not be too disappointed if it is lacking in our own.

The three zones are of the same height and have approximately the same width in the ideal face. In practice, however, it is commoner to find an equality of height rather than an equality of width, because the breadth of the zones is determined by the shape of the face and is only constant in those who possess either a square face or a rectangular face. Figure 45 shows how the zonal widths are affected by the face shape.

In general, the zone height symbolizes the intensity of the qualities linked with the zone, while its breadth serves as a measure of the steadfastness, resolution and openness associated with them. A high forehead, for example, signifies a quick, intelligent mind, while a broad forehead is indicative of wide interests and open views, the

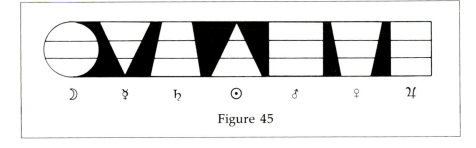

Figure 45

two together naturally suggesting a more knowledgeable and wiser mind. A low forehead, by contrast, represents a poorer intellect and slower mental processes, and a narrow forehead betokens limited interests and a restricted understanding, which when combined can often result in zealotry, bigotry, and, at worst, fanaticism.

In the upright triangle or Sun face there is a clear imbalance between the width of the Upper Zone and the Lower Zone, the former being narrow and the latter broad, which signifies a narrowness of view and a limited understanding combined with a restless and persistent energy. There is a similar imbalance in the inverted triangle or Mercury face, although the emphasis is reversed. In this case there is a broad, open mind associated with limited persistence and resolution, which is why those with such a face tend to be flighty, easily bored, and irresponsible. And although there is an equality of mental talent and energy in the round, or Moon-faced, type, which is to that person's advantage, neither is capable of supporting his or her adaptive abilities, which is why they are likely to feel frustrated and unfulfilled.

The square, or Mars, face does show an equality of breadth (and often of height) in its zones, which signifies inner balance and helps explain why those with such a face are usually able to achieve what they want. However, the zones of the Mars face are somewhat low in height, indicating a lack of sparkle and zest. This is why Mars-faced people tend to be slow, stolid and conservative, having personalities much like that of the god Mars in early myth, who was an agricultural deity worshipped by the Roman peasants. It was only later that Mars became the god of war and was thereby accredited with an aggressive, virile nature.

Both the truncated upright triangle, or Saturn, face and the amputated inverted triangle, or Venus, face show an improvement in overall balance when compared with the two face shapes they respectively resemble, the Sun face and the Mercury face. The Saturn face has a broader Upper Zone and its owner thus has a broader mind than does the Sun face type, while the Venus face has a wider Lower Zone, indicating greater application, than does the Mercury face. Hence it is not surprising to find that both types of person are better able to achieve their ambitions and so fulfill themselves than are their more restricted facial cousins.

The rectangular, or Jupiter, face displays the same equality of breadth as the Mars face, yet its zones enjoy a greater height. When the zones are both high and broad, which is what we find in the best Jupiter faces, they symbolize the development of intellect, adaptability and energy to their fullest capacity. This explains why those who rise to positions of power and influence tend to have Jupiter faces.

While the zones are more likely to show an equality of height than of breadth, they quite often vary in this respect. Differences in zone height reflect inner imbalances, as the increased activity or quickness of the character quality signified by the high zone is not matched by those that are low in height. For instance, a square-faced Mars person may have a high forehead, yet its height diminishes that of the other two zones, so that although he is probably highly intelligent, he is effectively disadvantaged by his shyness or lack of enthusiasm (signified by the deficient Lower Zone) and by his inability to cope with those obstacles and difficulties that he may encounter (suggested by the low Middle Zone). Such an individual will therefore find it hard to live happily or to gain personal fulfilment, unless he can meet up with a mentor who can guide and encourage him. Hence it is not surprising to discover that everyday life provides us with many examples of the modern Svengali, who earn their living dealing with the problems that baffle or terrify the talented yet insecure, or who take the opportunity of exploiting, as did Rasputin, those who are weaker than themselves, but who have wealth and power.

However, those with faces which have zones of equal height and have a straight mid-line, but whose zones differ in width, often become rich and successful. Consider, for example, the face of the film-star Dick Powell, shown in Figure 46.

Powell's hair-line, although it is somewhat uneven, runs straight across the top of his broad forehead, from which the sides of his face slope downwards and inwards to the relatively narrow, yet by no means pointed chin. This is an amputated inverted triangle, or Venus, face, a shape that is commonly possessed by those who work in the entertainment business. The Venus face is broadest across the forehead or Upper Zone, which in Powell's case is remarkably rectangular, somewhat narrower across the Middle Zone, and narrowest across the Lower Zone. If you now measure the length of his nose from its tip to the point immediately between the inner ends of his eyebrows, which constitutes the height of the Middle Zone, you will find that this distance exactly equals that of both the Upper Zone and the Lower Zone. Hence each zone has the ideal equality of height. And likewise, the mid-line running from the point of hair growing upon Powell's position 15 down to the centre of his chin is straight, passing as it does precisely down the middle of his nose and through the centre of his mouth.

Such straightness and balance contributed to Dick Powell's good looks, as did the shape and regularity of his features. But more importantly, from a physiognomical point of view, this evenness of form suggests that Powell would achieve something with his life, that he would not fail through want of intelligence, adaptability or energy,

Figure 46: Dick Powell   Figure 47: Nelson Eddy

even though he did not have sufficient of the latter to find success in a more demanding field than entertainment. But he made the right choice by opting to tread the boards, where he carved out a varied and rewarding career for himself.

Born in 1904, Dick Powell had musical talents which he was encouraged to develop as a child—he sang in a church choir—and which enabled him to make a living as a singer and musician in several bands during his late teens and 20s. Then, in 1932, he was spotted by a Warner Brothers' talent scout and given a small part in the film *Blessed Event*, which led to him being offered a long-term movie contract with the company. He subsequently sang and acted in many films, including seven made with Ruby Keeler, and was voted into the box-office top 10 list of movie stars for 1935 and 1936.

During the Second World War his desire for more substantial parts resulted in him being chosen to play Philip Marlowe in the film adaptation of Raymond Chandler's novel *Farewell, My Lovely* (*Murder, My Sweet*, 1945). Similar hard-bitten parts followed in films like *Johnny O'Clock* (1947) and *Pitfall* (1949), while in *The Reformer and the Redhead* (1950) he co-starred with his wife June Allyson (he had previously been married to Joan Blondell). But his declining popularity as a film star encouraged him to switch to television production in 1952, when he formed the Four Star Playhouse with David Niven and Charles Boyer. This was later transformed into Four Star Television, which made many popular TV shows, including 'The Dick Powell Show' in which he played a Marlowe-like private detective. It was a portrayal that earned Raymond Chandler's sarcastic comment: 'Stay tuned in for the Dick Powell Show. Starring (you guessed it) Dick Powell. The greatest private detective (that sings tenor)'. Powell made his last movie in 1954, the taut *Susan Slept Here*. He died of lung cancer in 1963.

But no face is perfect and Dick Powell's reveals certain flaws that mar its otherwise fortunate balance. It is helpful to identify the most important of these, although I shall leave it to the reader to discover their significance in the relevant chapters. For instance, Powell's hairline is uneven and indistinct; his forehead lacks well-defined creases; his eyebrows are set too close to his eyes; his irises float too high, revealing a glimpse of white beneath the right iris; his right cheekline is poorly formed; his philtrum is shallow and ill-defined; and his lips are dissimilar in thickness, the upper being thinner than the lower. No account can of course be given of his colouring from the original sepia print, nor can anything be said about those facial blemishes which might have been either covered by make-up or erased by the photographer.

It is pertinent to compare Dick Powell's face with that of Nelson Eddy (see Figure 47), who was his contemporary and who also achieved considerable popularity in films as a singer. Indeed, in many respects their lives were very similar.

Nelson Eddy was born in 1901. He sang, like Dick Powell, in church choirs as a boy, and later, while working as a journalist on a Philadelphia newspaper, performed in amateur musicals. This led, via a successfully-entered competition, to a place in the Philadelphia Civic Opera, with which he sang in a number of operas and recitals, including some radio broadcasts, that made him quite well-known. He was spotted by a film scout in 1933 and signed by MGM, although little use was at first made of him. His big chance came when he partnered Jeanette MacDonald in *Naughty Marietta* (1935), and its success encouraged the studio to make a second film featuring them both. This was the wildly popular *Rose Marie* (1936), which resulted in the two stars being called 'The Singing Sweethearts'. Further pictures together followed, the last of which was *I Married an Angel* (1942). After their split, Eddy's popularity as a movie star declined and he retired from film acting in 1947. He thereafter returned to making records and giving concerts, and made something of a come-back in the 1960s when he worked the night-club circuit. In fact he was singing one of his film favourites when he collapsed on stage and died of a stroke in 1967.

Nelson Eddy's face has the same Venus shape as that of Dick Powell's, although his narrower forehead, signifying a less open and versatile mind, makes it less easy to distinguish. The three facial zones share the same height, and the mid-line, taking into account the slight turn of his head, is straight. His full head of wavy hair is almost identical to Powell's, as is the essentially horizontal, yet uneven and imprecise, hair-line. His forehead lacks creases and his eyebrows, although not quite as low-set as Powell's, press too close to his eyes. (The reader may care to note that position 24 on Eddy's forehead is noticeably hollow, which suggests, along with the absence of horizontal forehead creases, and in spite of his forehead's height, that he wasn't the brightest of men). However, his irises are large, well-controlled and bright, and do not float too high. Indeed, his eyes are his best feature. They indicate that his most fortunate life period took place between the ages of 34 and 39. And indeed this was when he achieved his greatest success in films partnering Jeanette MacDonald. His nose, like Powell's, has the same straight Grecian bridge. His philtrum is similarly indistinct, and his upper lip is thinner than his lower. It is not possible to properly compare the cheeklines as both of Eddy's are obscured by shadow, although his right one appears to be quite distinctly marked.

These feature deficiencies, such as they are, combined with the similar positive characteristics, indicate that not only were the two men alike but that they would share broadly similar fates. Yet Powell, as his wider forehead reveals, had greater versatility, which is why he not only attempted more demanding film roles, but went on to direct and produce once he had retired from the screen. The less able Eddy stayed a singer and died in harness at age 66, whereas Powell, living more dangerously, gave up the ghost at age 59. But then Eddy's stronger chin suggests that he would have a longer life.

There are dangers, however, in attempting to analyse the characters and fates of the famous from photographs. We have already noted how make-up can be used to hide important markings or blemishes, or that these may have been deliberately erased by the photographer. And women not only normally wear make-up, but they frequently change their natural looks by plucking their eyebrows, wearing wigs, adding beauty spots and so on, as well as undergoing more radical alterations by having face-lifts and other surgical operations. Indeed, today's men are increasingly likely to alter their looks in this way, especially if they are in the public eye, which presents further problems for the face reader.

But it is fair to ask that, if the unaltered face accurately symbolizes the inner man or woman, might not the inner person be changed by a restructuring of the face? There can be no doubt that this is true, at least to a certain extent, particularly for those whose disproportionally large or improperly formed features have been causing them unhappiness and undermining their feelings of self-worth. And this in itself underlines the basic tenet of face reading, which says that the well-balanced face with regular, normally-sized features bespeaks a calm, honest and psychologically sound personality, whereas the opposite type of face belongs to the anxious, the unhappy, and the problematical. And while it is less likely that minor improvements, by using make-up, for example, can effect such changes of character, there is no doubt that skilfully applied make-up can temporarily boost a woman's confidence.

Chapter Six
THE EARS

'Since the brow often speaks true, since the eyes and noses have tongues, and the countenance proclaims the heart and inclinations, let observation so far instruct thee in physiognomical lines as to be some rule for thy distinction, and guide for thy affection unto such as look most like men.'

From *Christian Morals* by Sir Thomas Browne.

The ears, by their position, shape and colour, say much about our inner selves and should not be ignored, despite the fact that their observation in others is often made difficult by their being hidden by the hair. Indeed, such reticence in displaying the ears may be caused by an intuitive knowledge of their significance.

The bendable outer flaps that we commonly call the ears are known to scientists as *pinnae* and serve merely to direct sound waves into the ear hole and thus to the ear-drum, from whence three small bones, the auditory ossicles, relay its vibrations across the middle ear to the inner ear, where they are converted into nerve impulses and conveyed by the auditory nerve to the hearing centres of the brain. The pinnae are constructed of flexible cartilage, which is overlain by skin. Their movement is rudimentary in man, although in other mammals they can be accurately turned and directed to catch the slightest sounds.

The size and appearance of the outer ears differ greatly from person to person, and indeed they are unique to the individual. In fact this led to the suggestion, before the introduction of fingerprinting, that they should be used to identify criminals. But earprinting would have been of little use in criminal detection, as law-breakers seldom apply their ears to surfaces at the scene of the crime.

Each pinna or ear has a rather complicated structure, which is illustrated in Figure 48. The outer rim of the ear, which normally curls

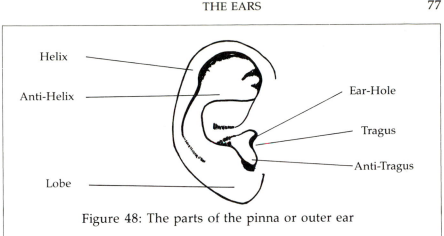

Figure 48: The parts of the pinna or outer ear

over somewhat to form a flange, is called the *helix*, and the convolutions lying within it are known as the *anti-helix*. The *tragus* is the small nodule which projects backwards across the opening of the ear hole, beneath which is a downward scoop resembling a bay, known as the *anti-tragus*. At the base of the pinna lies the fleshy *lobe*, to which ear-rings can be attached.

As far as dating is concerned, your ears symbolize the earliest years of your life, the left ear representing your first six years of existence, the right ear the following seven years. Your left ear also symbolizes your relationship with your father, and your right ear that with your mother. However, the Chinese claim that the opposite is true for women—i.e. that their left ear signifies the mother and the right ear the father. Hence if both ears are badly formed this is a sure sign of an unhappy childhood and of difficulties with both parents. If only one ear is abnormal—by sticking out, for example, while the other lies close to the side of the head—then it reveals problems with the parent signified by that ear and which caused particular unhappiness at the time of life represented by the ear.

Your ears also stand for certain character traits, which are discussed below, as well as auguring, along with the eyes and nose, which likewise lie in the Middle Zone of the face, your fortunes in middle life. Lastly, each part of the ears can be linked with a specific area of the body, a fact that is taken advantage of in acupuncture.

The position of your ears on the sides of your head gives a simple, yet accurate, guide to your intelligence. However, they need to be examined from both the front and from the side. The average ears, when viewed from the front, lie within the Middle Zone, their tops level with, or perhaps slightly higher than, the eyes (see Figure 49). Ears having such a placement signify an average intelligence.

The higher your ears are set, or the closer their tops come to the

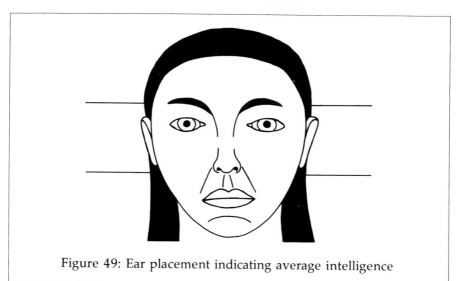

Figure 49: Ear placement indicating average intelligence

eyebrows, the greater is your intelligence. Indeed, the ideal ears are large, extending from the eyebrows to the bottom of the nose, and they lie flat against the sides of the head, have a good shape, and a colour that is lighter than the face. Such ears—and you are lucky if yours are like this—symbolize the person who is very clever, modest, and fortunate.

If the tops of your ears are set on a higher level than your eyebrows, you have a superior intellect and will in all probability rise to a position of some importance in life. But unfortunately, high-set ears also betoken a difficult and demanding personality, which means, should you have such ears, that you like your own way and have scant regard for the feelings of others. Yet your nature is less unpleasant if your ear lobes reach down as far as the base of your nose and if your ears have the positive characteristics mentioned in the previous paragraph. But if your ears, no matter what their height, have a dark red colour, stick out and lack a good shape, then you are a very difficult and possibly violent person.

Conversely, when the ears fail to reach the level of the eyes, they signify an intellectually inferior person. And when low-set ears lack an incurved helix, they further reveal that their owner has no confidence and little self-esteem. Hence he is unlikely to make much of his life.

The ears should ideally be set on the same level, but in practice it is usual to find one lying slightly above the other. It is never a good sign when the ears are obviously lopsided as this robs the face of balance. Lopsided ears suggest that the early years were unhappy and unstable, quite possibly because the parents had a poor marriage, the

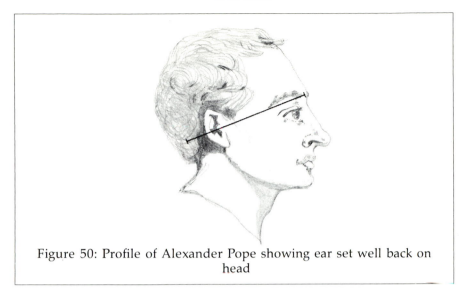

Figure 50: Profile of Alexander Pope showing ear set well back on head

child suffering as a result. The degree of psychological damage is shown by the other ear features. If the ears are large, lie flat against the sides of the head, have a pale colour and a good shape—which are all positive features—they indicate that the person concerned adjusted tolerably well to his childhood difficulties and used, or will use, the energies they created to advance himself. But when badly lopsided ears have one or more other negative features, then the psychological trauma was great and deep, and may blight the life. However, such ears must be read with the rest of the face, as their indications may be moderated by other strongly-formed and well-balanced features.

When examining your ears from the side, their position must be referred to an imaginary line drawn from a point between your eyebrows, through the ear hole, and to the back of your neck (see Figure 50).

If the distance in front of your ear is two-thirds of the total—and we are evaluating your face as a two-dimensional profile—it signifies that you have an average amount of intelligence. A greater proportion symbolizes a higher intelligence, which is necessarily linked to it. For example, in the profile shown in Figure 50, which is that of Alexander Pope (1688–1744), there is a noticeably larger distance forward of the ear hole—approaching three-quarters of the total—which suggest a very high intelligence indeed. This estimate is supported by the large ears, which extend from slightly below the long nose to between the eyes and the eyebrow, and by the high, wide forehead. Pope is one of England's greatest poets and the author of those celebrated lines that are so relevant to our present study:

'Know then thyself, presume not God to scan;
The proper study of mankind is Man.'

When the distance in front of the ears is less than two-thirds of the total, the intelligence is proportionally lower, while the animal traits, which are signified by the distance behind the ears, are proportionally greater. Thus should the ears lie mid-way along the line joining the base of the forehead with the back of the neck, the person concerned has strong animal drives and a weak intellect, unless his face displays contrary features.

But clearly, because there are three principal indicators of intelligence, viz. a) the height and breadth of the forehead, b) the height of the ears, and c) the placement of the ear hole, it is necessary to take all three into account before reaching a judgment. When each suggests a superior intellect, as they do in the case of Alexander Pope, then we can be quite sure that the person is intellectually gifted. But when their indications are mixed, the true IQ is likely to fall somewhere between the two greatest extremes. For instance, there is just such a mixture in the photograph of the young Cary Grant shown in Figure 51.

Grant's forehead is quite high, if not all that broad, and the distance before his ear-hole compared to that behind it is in the ratio of two-

Figure 51: Cary Grant   Figure 52: Clark Gable

thirds to one-third, which together suggest an average or slightly above average intelligence. Yet if we also take into account the size of his ear, whose top lies on the same level as his eyebrows and whose lobe reaches down to the bottom of his nose, we must necessarily upgrade his intellectual level, if not to superior, then certainly to well above average. This being so, it comes as no surprise to discover that Grant, according to David Shipman in *The Great Movie Stars* (1979), 'was unique among Hollywood stars in handling his own business activities; and he had full control over every aspect of the films he made'. And such successful self-guidance made Cary Grant into a multi-millionaire.

The best type of ears can be seen from the front, but lie almost flat against the sides of the head (see Figure 46). Such visible yet by no means obvious ears signify both a happy childhood and a successful and contented middle-age.

However, if the ears lie so close to the sides of the head that they cannot be seen from the front, they betoken a person who was over-protected as a child, and who, as a result, has developed into a lazy and irresponsible adult. He or she is likely to be an indifferent employee and marriage partner, and is therefore at a disadvantage in life. Yet if the facial features are well-formed and in balance with each other, he will gain more energy and resolution as he ages, although he may never become fully mature.

Ears that stick out from the sides of the head are symbolic of an unhappy childhood—the degree of unhappiness being directly related to the amount of lateral extension—which throws a shadow over the life. They also presage a difficult and often unhappy middle-age. School children with projecting or 'jug' ears are frequently disruptive, their bad behaviour stemming from their troubled home life, and not, as the cynic might claim, from the fact that they are made unhappy by their outstanding ears. Indeed, we have already noted that projecting ears are one of the signs, according to Cesare Lombroso, of a criminal nature.

But when ears that stick out are partnered by facial features which represent character strengths, the energies unleashed by the difficult childhood can be generally directed into positive channels in later life, thereby enriching and making more successful the adult years. Clark Gable, the late King of Hollywood, is perhaps the best-known celebrity who had outstanding ears (see Figure 52).

Gable, an only child, was born at Cadiz, Ohio, on 1 February 1901. His mother Adeline died when he was nine months old. He was reared by his father, William Gable, a tough oil driller who despised actors and their kind. Yet when he remarried, the young Clark gained support from his stepmother, who encouraged his artistic dreams.

There can be no doubt that Gable rose above his troubled childhood and became a wealthy and much-loved film star, despite the fact that he developed a mother-fixation. His first wife, Josephine Dillon, a drama coach whom he met while working as a telephone repair man, was 17 years his senior, and his second wife, the heiress Rita Langham, was his elder by 14 years. A more conventional relationship was next begun with Carole Lombard—she was born in 1908—yet their 1939 marriage took place during his negative middle-life period, revealed by his projecting ears, and was ended when she was tragically killed in a plane crash in 1942. Gable was devastated by her death and never fully recovered from it. He briefly married another older woman, Sylvia, Lady Ashley, before finally settling down with the youthful Kay Spreckles, who bore him his only child, a son, shortly after he died in 1960, having just completed work on *The Misfits* with Marilyn Monroe.

The size of the ears is also important. They should ideally be large yet in proportion with the other features, as were Clark Gable's. Small ears belong to the slow-witted and easily-led person, who finds it hard to keep out of trouble. Very large ears likewise rob the face of balance. They reveal that their owner is immature, displaying childish traits like greed, sulkiness and selfishness, which negatively affect his relationships. In fact Aristotle himself said of large ears: 'Great and thick ears are a certain sign of a foolish person.' To which he added, 'Ears sticking out and extremely large indicate stupidity, garrulity and imprudence.'

If the top of your ears are rounded in shape it shows you have an open and enthusiastic nature, whereas if they are flattened you are a more controlled type, who functions best in a settled and structured environment. Pointed ears are negative in meaning, being indicative of a selfish, demanding, and sometimes aggressive, person. These tendencies are at their worst when the ears are thin and lacking in body.

The form of the helix or outer flange of the ears reveals much about how we view ourselves and how we impinge on the world. This is why we must consider their appearance in some detail.

It is never a favourable sign when the helices of the ears are flat, as this signifies weakly developed or even entirely absent qualities of character. Nor is it good when the helices are so tightly curled that they form a tube, a development that represents an unnatural accentuation of the characteristics symbolized by the helices. Those with rolled helices tend therefore to have grandiose ideas about themselves and a strong desire to persuade others to think like them. They can do great harm when their beliefs are misguided or evil.

The helix of each ear can be divided into five zones that are arranged around it like the hours on a clock. However, the zones often run into one another without any limiting break or indentation, which makes their exact beginning and end hard to locate. Yet it is quite common to find that one or other of the zones is emphasized in different people, a development which reflects some of their differences in character.

Zone 1 marks the start of the helix at the side of the head (see Figure 53). It is frequently the broadest and most obvious of the zones, and when it is well-formed it signifies a strong ego and an accompanying pride in oneself. Indeed, such people wish to advance themselves in the world and thereby attract the attention of others. This explains why those in the public eye invariably have a well-developed Zone 1 on their ears. Personal pride, however, is sadly lacking in those without this zone, who may be regarded as having an inferiority complex, and it is only present in a limited form in those persons who have an obvious Zone 1 on one ear but not the other.

Zone 2 lies at the apex of the helix (see Figure 54) and when well-developed it betokens strongly-held ideas or convictions. If it is partnered by a weakly formed or absent Zone 1, these ideas may manifest as harmless eccentricities, but when they are united with a strong ego, signified by a well-formed Zone 1, they naturally give a purpose and a direction to the life. If Zone 2 is rolled over into a tube, it shows that the convictions are based on illogical premises and may, if the other facial features have a negative cast, be used to justify bigotry and other extreme notions. Should Zone 2 be less well-developed on one ear than the other, then the beliefs are not so fervently held.

Zone 3 comprises the start of the downward bend of the helix of

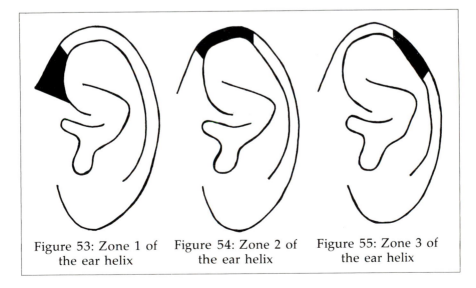

Figure 53: Zone 1 of   Figure 54: Zone 2 of   Figure 55: Zone 3 of
the ear helix   the ear helix   the ear helix

each ear (see Figure 55). When this zone is well-formed it represents an inborn curiosity about everything that is at all odd or mysterious, especially that which has the so-called experts scratching their heads. Hence those with a pair of accentuated Zone 3's enjoy reading about and investigating topics like UFOs, Atlantis, Eldorado, ESP, life after death, etc., as well as the oddities of science, and if they also have noticeable Zone 2's they will have plenty of their own ideas about such things. Well-developed Zone 1's will mark out the person who is directly involved in either eccentric research or in mounting an expedition. A rolled-over Zone 3 betrays the person with a bee in his bonnet.

Zone 4, the longest of the five, forms the outer edge of the ear and is directed downwards towards the lobe (see Figure 56). It signifies the power of concentration and of continuance, hence when it is well-developed it identifies the person who sticks at a task until it is completed or at a problem until it is solved. This is particularly true of those whose Zone 4 runs without interruption from Zone 3 to Zone 5. Such people never give up. If the zone is found on one ear but not on the other, the imbalance represents a person who was either clever as a child but a failure in later life, or who, like Winston Churchill and Albert Einstein, was regarded as a dunce when young but who developed into a highly talented adult.

Zone 5, when present, runs into the ear lobe. It symbolizes a material turn of mind and hence a preoccupation with money and all that it can buy. Those with clearly visible Zone 5's believe that clothes and comforts make the man or woman, which is why they constantly scramble to not only keep up with, but to exceed, the Joneses. Yet

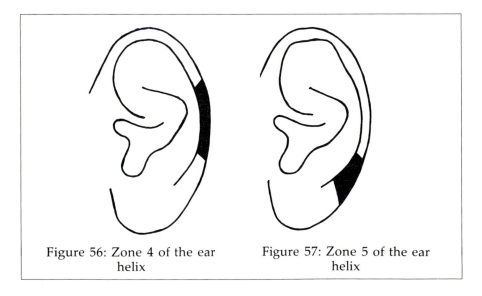

Figure 56: Zone 4 of the ear helix

Figure 57: Zone 5 of the ear helix

they are not entirely selfish and when possessed of larger ideas may actively help to bring the material benefits of life to more people.

The lobe of the ear is very important, as it can reveal much about a person's character, longevity and fate. You should therefore examine your own with care.

It was long ago realized that each ear bears a close resemblance to an about-to-be-born foetus. As such, the lobe corresponds to the foetus's head, which helps explain why mental qualities are associated with it. It is also the reason why acupuncturists place needles in the ear lobe to cure head problems.

The best and most fortunate ear lobes are large, rounded and plump. If your ear lobes are so formed, then you not only have a clever mind and great understanding, but also advanced spiritual qualities. Indeed, the Buddha was said to have ear lobes of such size that they reached down to his shoulders. Large lobes also signify the rise to a high position in life, although such a prediction can only be made when they are accompanied by other positive features. This is why Cesare Lombroso found that born criminals often had abnormally large ear lobes; these typically grew from very large ears that were out of balance with the rest of the face. Large ear lobes are also one sign of a long life. The reader may have noticed that very old people always have large ear lobes.

The SDP leader Dr David Owen has large ear lobes (see Figure 58) and these reflect the success he has achieved in politics and his unique grasp of both national and foreign affairs. And yet the coming few years are likely to be disappointing for him. He reached the age of 51 on 2 July 1989, and the following four years (1989–1993) are

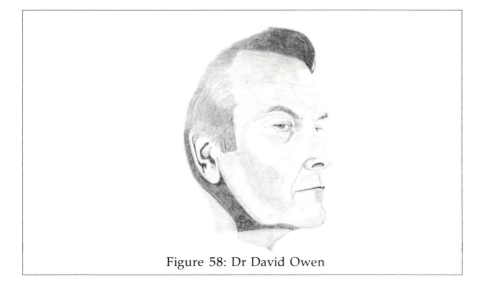

Figure 58: Dr David Owen

symbolized by his thin lips, his worst facial feature. He can thus expect to be left out in the cold for some time yet.

Smaller ear lobes necessarily represent a mind of more modest understanding and a less spectacular fortune. But lobes that are too thin, even if they are large, are robbed of their promise by their lack of substance. So too are lobes that grow into the sides of the face, which are not, in other words, free-hanging.

Ears without lobes are the most unfortunate. They signify trivial thought processes, base pleasures, difficulties in getting ahead, and a short life. This is why Lombroso also noted that many criminals have ears without lobes.

It is never a good sign when hair grows from either the ear hole or, worse still, from the pinna itself. Visible hair undermines the value of the ear's strong points, showing that the talents are not exploited. Hair growing on inferior ears together symbolize a base character and an unfortunate life.

Chapter Seven
THE FOREHEAD

'Her yvorie forehead, full of bountie brave,
Like a broad table did it selfe dispred,
For Love his loftie triumphs to engrave,
And write the battailes of his great godhed:
All good and honour might therein be red,
For there their dwelling was.'

From *The Faerie Queen* by Edmund Spenser.

The forehead, as we have already discovered, forms the Upper Zone of the face. It represents the powers of the intellect and those traits of character associated with them. It also symbolizes a person's fate between the ages of 15 and 29.

The shape of the forehead is largely determined by the hair-line. The hair-line may run across the top of the forehead in a straight line, or it may arch upwards to form a semi-circle or a point, or it may droop downwards to describe an M-shape. These different hair-lines not only modify the meaning of the forehead, but they also contribute to the overall shape of the face.

The forehead height is measured from the point between the eyebrows to the hair-line. This distance should ideally be equal to the length of the nose and to the height of the Lower Zone. It is never a good sign if the forehead is lower in height than either of these two zones, as it reveals a low intelligence and a lack of mental sparkle.

A high forehead, on the other hand, is indicative of both a high intelligence and a ready wit. But the forehead should not noticeably exceed the height of either of the two lower zones. If it does it betokens troubled thought processes and an inability to get along with other people.

Figure 59: Sir Walter Raleigh

had uneven hair-lines, although the latter's was less pronounced, but both went on to become famous singers and film stars.

'He was a tall, handsome, and bold man; but his blemish was that he was damnably proud,' wrote John Aubrey of Sir Walter Raleigh, adding: 'He had a most remarkable aspect, an exceedingly high forehead, and sour eye-lided, a kind of pig eye' (see Figure 59).

However, it is important not to overestimate the forehead height of men with a receding hair-line. Loss of hair does not heighten the true forehead, whose upper border can always be detected on close examination. As a rough guide the forehead should not be less than two inches in height or greater than three and a half inches in height.

The forehead width is determined by measuring the distance from the hairline of one temple to that of the other, one inch above the eyebrows (see Figure 60). Although the forehead width is naturally determined by the size of the skull, for guidance we can say that a wide forehead has a breadth of at least six inches.

The forehead width, as was explained in Chapter Five, symbolizes a person's breadth of view and degree of understanding, which are greater if the forehead is wide and less if it is narrow. A narrow forehead is typically formed when the hair grows forwards on the temples, such as we see in the picture of Junzo Okudairo (see Figure 5) and which is symbolic of his criminal fanaticism. Such forward growing hair is also present on the temples of Margaret Thatcher whose forehead, while high, is comparatively narrow (see Figure 61). This suggests that although the Prime Minister is a woman of considerable intelligence, she has rather narrow or restricted views. Yet

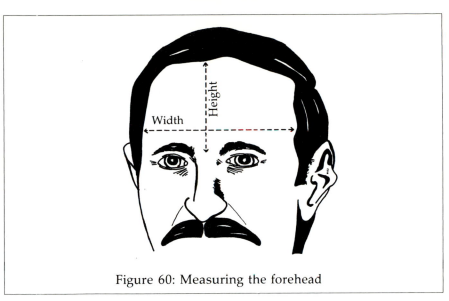

Figure 60: Measuring the forehead

unlike Junzo Okudairo, Mrs Thatcher has otherwise excellent facial features, which signify both high office and a long life.

The temples are formed by the forehead falling back above the

Figure 61: Mrs Margaret Thatcher, the Prime Minister

ends of the eyebrows, the two corners of which should be gently rounded, not angular like steps. Rounded corners bring out the best in whatever positive characteristics the forehead may show, whereas angular corners worsen the meaning of a forehead's good features, while adding yet another dour indication to a forehead that is low or narrow or otherwise poorly formed.

When the hair-line is straight, which it typically is if the face shape is square or rectangular, or like that of an inverted triangle or an amputated inverted triangle (i.e., Mars, Jupiter, Mercury and Venus faces), it signifies a rational mind, the sort which belongs to the person who thinks rather than feels and who believes that all human problems can be solved by brain power. This type is thus practical and methodical in his approach to life.

A straight hair-line is also usually possessed by those with a truncated upright triangle or Saturn face (see Figure 63), although its length is shortened by the forward-growing hair on the temples.

A short, straight hair-line symbolizes a repressed personality with its accompanying bad temper and irritability, limited tastes and interests, and decided views. Such people have often had an unhappy childhood and thus tend to be starved of affection, yet because their sex urge is strong, they may mistake sex for love and so marry early in life, with often disastrous results, or they may not marry at all, preferring instead to take one lover after another. Hence they are typically anxious and prone to depression.

A rounded hair-line generally accompanies a round or Moon face (see Figure 64), when it may be said to symbolize the fickleness, superstition, and over-imagination characteristic of this type, but when it forms part of another face shape, it signifies a more open and intuitive mind, and hence a greater individuality. The owner of a

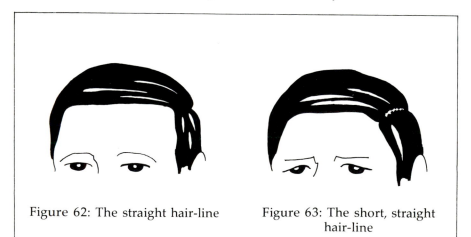

Figure 62: The straight hair-line   Figure 63: The short, straight hair-line

rounded hair-line thus tends to be somewhat irresponsible and difficult to live with, selfish and fond of good living, which in turn engenders exploitative and money-grabbing behaviour.

The peaked hair-line typically belongs to the upright triangle or Sun face (see Figure 65), although it is more often found in a less pointed form. It betokens troubled teenage years and is therefore the mark of an insecure and somewhat inadequate person, who wishes to separate himself from his despised roots and rise in the world, often under an assumed name. The intelligence is high but the views are narrow, which is why the lower sort is attracted to extreme and often violent revolutionary groups. These offer him emotional acceptance and 'love' and also the opportunity of getting even with society.

The M-shaped hair-line symbolizes the artist, the type who is not only sensitive to line, form and colour, but who also wants to be applauded and acclaimed (see Figure 66). This person feels different from and superior to those around him, whose tastes and aspirations he commonly derides, but whose help he welcomes when the going gets tough. Such people prefer to live a free existence and do not want to be encumbered with responsibility. They will tell their public that they love them, but in fact they only love themselves.

A jagged or uneven hair-line (see Figure 67) belongs to the rebellious, neurotic, and ill-humoured person, who is at odds with the society in which he lives, and who, as a result of his attitudes and behaviour, had a difficult and unhappy youth. However, such 'outsider' tendencies are not necessarily a handicap to finding success, and indeed if the forehead itself is high and broad, then he will rise above his early troubles and make something of his life. For example, both Nelson Eddy (see Figure 47) and Dick Powell (see Figure 46)

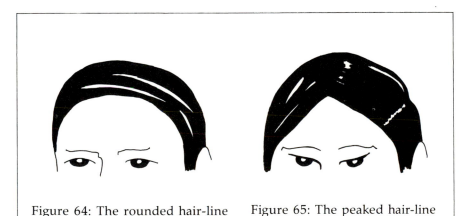

Figure 64: The rounded hair-line   Figure 65: The peaked hair-line

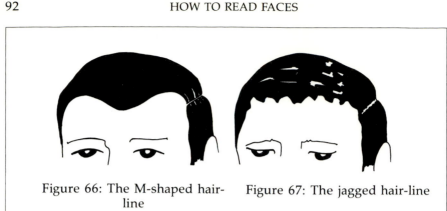

Figure 66: The M-shaped hair-
line

Figure 67: The jagged hair-line

It is important, when evaluating your own forehead, to examine it from the side as well as from the front. But before we consider the forehead in profile, it is first necessary to mention the work of the Dutch anatomist and naturalist Petrus Camper (1722–1789), whose celebrated essay titled *The Connexion between the Science of Anatomy and The Arts of Drawing, Painting, Statuary, etc., etc.* (1781) disclosed the link he had discovered between the position of the forehead relative to the lips, when seen in profile view, and the degree of beauty and the amount of intelligence displayed by the person concerned. He wrote:

'When in addition to the skull of a negro, I had procured one of a Calmuck, and had placed that of an ape contiguous to them both, I observed that a line, drawn along the forehead and the upper lip, indicated this difference in national physiognomy; and also pointed out the degree of similarity between a negroe [sic] and the ape. By sketching some of these features upon a horizontal plane, I obtained the lines which mark the countenance, with their different angles. When I made these lines incline forwards, I obtained the face of an antique (i.e. a classical Greek): backwards, of a negro; still more backwards, the lines which mark an ape, a dog, a snipe, etc—This discovery formed the basis of my edifice.'

The now famous 'Camper's angle' is that made between a line drawn from the lips to the forehead (MG in Figure 68) and a horizontal line drawn through the ear-hole (AB in Figure 68). Camper found that the angle measured 47 degrees in the pongo, 58 degrees in the orang-utang, 70 degrees in the above-mentioned 'negroe' and Calmuck, and varied from a minimum of 70 degrees to a maximum of 80 degrees in his fellow Dutchmen, although it was normally larger in classical Greek profiles, such as those he examined in ancient coins, intaglios, mosaics, statues, etc.

'The two extremities of the facial line,' he noted, 'are from 70 degrees to 100 degrees, from the negro to the Grecian antique; make it under 70, and you describe the orang-utang or an ape: lessen it still more, and you have the head of a dog . . . (but) if the projecting part of the forehead be made to exceed the 100th degree the head becomes misshapen, and assumes the appearance of the hydrocephalus, or watery head.'

Hence Camper's hypothesis was that the greater the angle, always providing it did not exceed 100 degrees, the higher the intelligence and the more beautiful the face. Yet it is only fair to point out that, where negroes are concerned, Camper's measurements were limited to a single skull belonging to a member of this race, and that of an 11-year-old-boy ('I dissected the body of this youth publicly at Amsterdam, in the year 1758').

The interested reader may care to measure 'Camper's angle' on the profile of Alexander the Great (see Figure 31), which is large, and compare it with his own. If your angle approaches or perhaps equals that of Alexander, who was not only a brilliant military strategist—he conquered most of the known world—but who was also worshipped as a god in his lifetime, then it may be that your fate will prove as spectacular. This was certainly true of Elvis Presley (see Figure 69), whose profile angle was as large as, if not slightly greater than, Alexander's. Elvis conquered the world as the King of Rock 'n' Roll, and was—in fact, I believe, still is—worshipped as a god.

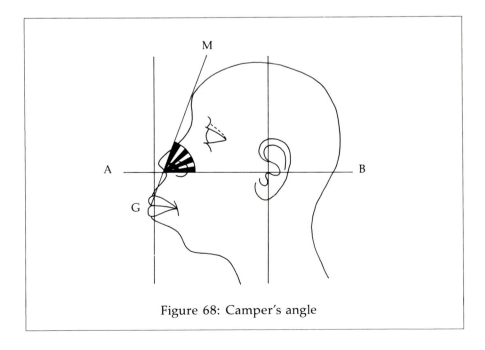

Figure 68: Camper's angle

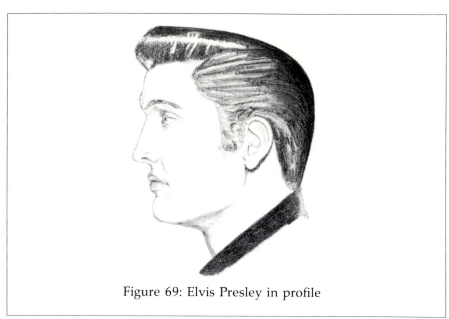

Figure 69: Elvis Presley in profile

But don't be too disappointed if your profile angle is smaller. The good fortune portended by a large angle seems limited to the years covered by the forehead, after which things take a decided turn for the worse. Alexander the Great died at the age of 32—he may have been poisoned—and Elvis Presley, after a long decline, at age 42.

The forehead can be divided horizontally into three regions (see Figure 70), each of which relates to particular mental faculties. When one or other of these is more pronounced, it reveals that the associated faculties are better developed.

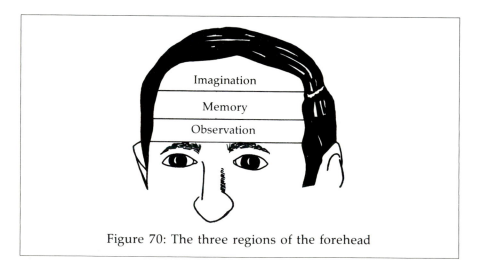

Figure 70: The three regions of the forehead

Should the area immediately above the eyebrows be fuller, the observational or perceptive abilities are keen (see Figure 71). If your own forehead shows such an enlargement, then not only will you have good eyesight, but you will notice details and respond to visual clues that the average person would miss. You will therefore excel at work requiring such skills, whether this be as mundane as inspecting finished articles for faults before they leave the factory, or as out-of-the-ordinary as tracking, spying and criminal detection. And good observation is needed for hobbies like bird-watching, clay-pigeon shooting and nature study, and of course for face reading and other methods of analysing character.

'It is said that you can tell a man's character from the way he wears his hat,' said Lord Baden-Powell, who was a skilled tracker and spy. 'If it is worn slightly on one side, the wearer is good natured; if it is worn very much on one side, he is a swaggerer; if on the back of his head, he is bad at paying his debts; if worn straight on top, he is probably honest, but very dull.'

If the middle region of your forehead is larger, so that it bulges out somewhat (see Figure 72) it reveals that you have a good memory, to the extent that you retain facts and other information that you see or hear with ease, although it does not mean that you are necessarily cleverer than someone with a poor memory. But as every type of memory can be improved with practice, there is no need to despair if yours resembles a sieve.

Lastly, if the upper portion of your forehead is prominent, it shows that you have an active imagination (see Figure 73). But while a good imagination is helpful to you if you work in a creative field, it can also make you over-sensitive to slights and likely to exaggerate difficulties,

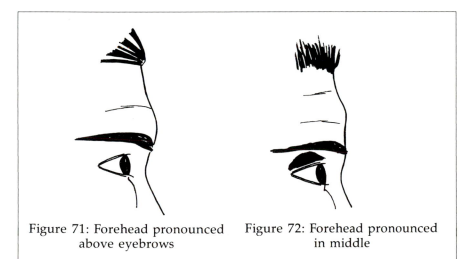

Figure 71: Forehead pronounced above eyebrows   Figure 72: Forehead pronounced in middle

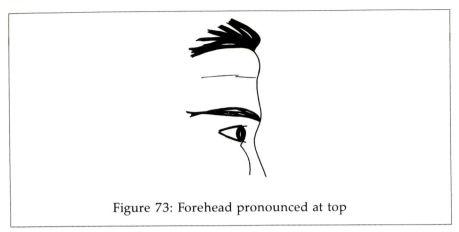

Figure 73: Forehead pronounced at top

as well as predisposing you to depression. A less prominent or flat upper forehead symbolizes a weaker imagination, and a receding upper region is the mark of someone with little or no imagination.

It is not a good sign if the forehead slopes sharply back or if it slopes forward or bulges above the eyes, for both conditions can indicate a low intelligence and mental instability. However, caution is required before making such an evaluation because another feature, such as the position of the ears, may tell a different story. For example, the photograph of Cary Grant (see Figure 51) reveals that his forehead sloped back quite sharply, yet his other, much more positive, facial features indicate that he was, despite this, both successful and *compos mentis*. Likewise, Julius Capitolinus tells us that the Roman emperor Verus 'was a tall man, and his forehead projected somewhat above his eyebrows . . . (but) he lived forty-two years, and ruled as Emperor, with his brother, for eleven.'

We have already spoken in an earlier chapter of those forehead creases that rise vertically above the nose, and we must now examine those that run horizontally across it. But first, some poetry:

'The seas are quiet when the winds give o'er;
So calm are we when passions are no more.
For then we know how vain it was to boast
Of fleeting things, so certain to be lost.
Clouds of affection from our younger eyes
Conceal that emptiness which age descries.

The soul's dark cottage, batter'd and decay'd,
Lets in new light through chinks that Time hath made:
Stronger by weakness, wiser men become
As they draw near to their eternal home.
Leaving the old, both worlds at once they view
That stands upon the threshold of the new.'

This poem, titled 'Old Age', was written by the seventeenth-century poet and royalist Edmund Waller, who was thus described by John Aubrey: 'He is of somewhat above middle stature, thin body, not at all robust; fine thin skin, his face somewhat of an olive complexion; his hair frizzed, of brownish colour; full eye, popping out and working; oval faced, his forehead high and *full of wrinkles . . .'*

Waller was exceptional, not only for his poetry, but for the fact that he lived be be 82 years old, when the average age at death was about 40. Hence we should not be surprised to learn that his forehead was 'full of wrinkles', as these have long been regarded as a sign of both venerableness and longevity. In fact no one of any worth who lives to an advanced age lacks forehead creases; it is only the slow-witted and callow, and the short-lived that do. And while the forehead creases deepen and more emphatically establish themselves as we grow older, they invariably appear, if they are ever going to, by our mid-twenties.

The interpretation of the forehead and its creases, an art known as metoposcopy, was perfected by the Italian savant Gerolamo Cardano, who wrote a number of books about it. Cardano claimed that the forehead typically bore up to seven horizontal creases, each of which he associated with one of the seven planets of traditional astrology. Starting at the top of the forehead and moving downwards, the creases are respectively ruled by Saturn, Jupiter, Mars, the Sun, Venus, Mercury, and the Moon (see Figure 74).

The creases are judged in a similar way to the lines of the palm. They are examined with regard to their number, clarity, length, colour, course, and depth, with special attention being given to negative

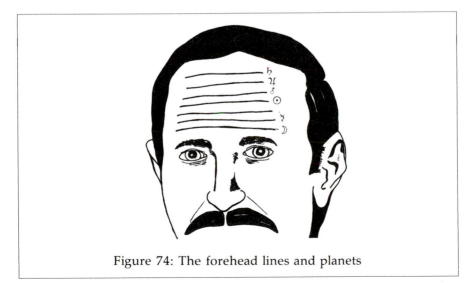

Figure 74: The forehead lines and planets

defects like breaks, islands, interceptive warts or moles, etc. But perhaps most importantly, they are held to symbolize planetary influences.

In this latter respect the forehead, which is said to be ruled by the zodiac sign of Aries, is analogous to the first house of the birth chart, whose natural sign ruler is Aries. The first house is primarily concerned with the self: it governs the appearance, the physical constitution, the temperament, and also, at least according to some astrologers, one's social status and fame. The creases of the forehead are thus read as planets in the first house would be, which explains why a forehead without creases is symbolic of a person with little character or personal force. Hence each crease adds to the individual whose forehead it decorates those traits linked with the planet that rules it, thereby rounding out the character and giving it greater depth.

However, it is not simply a case of the more creases, the better the person, because once the forehead creases reach a certain number, the planetary influences start interfering with each other and so have a negative effect. This is why Edmund Waller, whose forehead was 'full of wrinkles', was described by Aubrey as 'apt to be choleric'. Indeed, three long, well-marked and unbroken creases are the most fortunate to have, while five, six, or at worst, seven creases represent more problems for their owner than blessings. In fact a person with seven forehead creases is typically poor, ignorant and lonely. But at the other extreme, one well-marked, long and unbroken crease is a more positive sign than two or three faint, short, or broken creases. This is why Clark Gable, whose forehead bore two well-etched creases (see Figure 52), became a successful film star.

It is not always easy to tell which forehead crease is ruled by which planet, but if a crease runs across the brow mid-way between the eye-

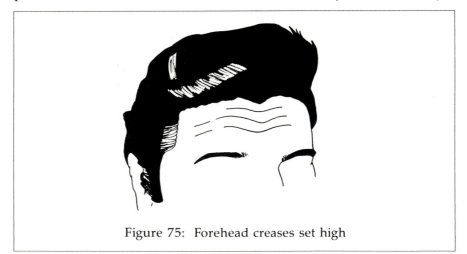

Figure 75: Forehead creases set high

brows and the hair-line, it can with confidence be linked with the Sun. Such a crease signifies a strong solar influence upon the person, which if not greatly modified by other planetary influences, will give a blond colouring, a strong physique, good health, an optimistic out-look, and plenty of energy. Those creases, if any, which lie above the mid-line are respectively ruled by Mars, Jupiter and Saturn, and those below by Venus, Mercury and the Moon.

The famous forehead shown in Figure 75 has its three fortunate creases set high. But while the lowest of these can be identified with the Sun, and the one closest to the hair-line with Saturn, it is difficult to say if the middle crease is ruled by Mars or Jupiter. However, because Presley ruined his health by excessive eating and by drug taking, and because Jupiter is the planet of over-indulgence, it is likely to be Jupiter.

The forehead shown in Figure 76 belongs to the English actor John Thaw, which is why the deeply marked, yet broken and waver-ing crease, placed a little below the mid-line, is ruled by Venus. Venus is the planetary significator of dancing, acting and other forms of entertainment, and governs a person's talents for these.

The third forehead, owned by celebrated writer Roald Dahl, shows a full complement of the lower creases (see Figure 77). The lowest complete crease is ruled by Mercury, which governs creative thought, writing and communication in general, and is typically seen on the foreheads of those who live by their pens. The full crease above it is ruled by Venus.

This forehead displays a variant of the lowest or Moon-ruled crease. When it is divided into two, as here, the half above the left eye is specifically ascribed to the Moon, while that above the right eye is said to be governed by the Sun, as illustrated in the

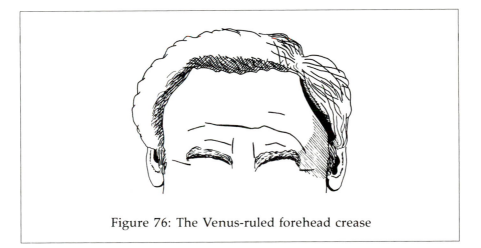

Figure 76: The Venus-ruled forehead crease

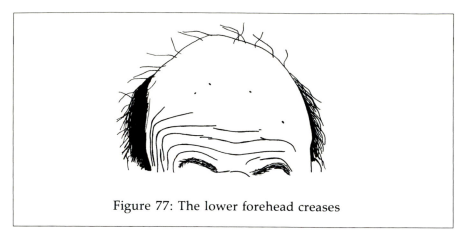

Figure 77: The lower forehead creases

ancient diagram shown in Figure 78.

The forehead creases have a positive meaning when they are long and unbroken, of good colour, and unaffected by warts or moles. They should also have a symmetrical wave shape, dipping down somewhat at their middle towards the nose, such as we see in Figure 75. When so formed, the lowermost Moon line denotes a good intuition, artistic sensitivity, a love of poetry and the sea, and luck with liquids; the second line, that of Mercury, reveals quick thought processes, verbal fluency, writing talents, and a flair for business; the third line, which is ruled by Venus, indicates a love of pleasure and the comforts of life, a good singing voice and musical talents, an ease of manner, and a talent for buying and selling; the fourth line, ruled by the Sun, signifies personal pride, a dignified manner and carriage,

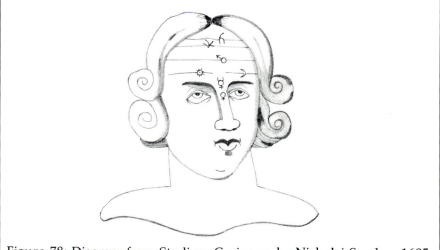

Figure 78: Diagram from Studium Curiosum by Nicholai Spadon, 1695

a desire for power and prestige, and a respect for law and order; the fifth line, that of Mars, is the sign of a hot temper, selfishness, and aggression, traits which cause conflict with others, but also great energy, courage and stamina, and a pioneering spirit; the sixth line, belonging to Jupiter, denotes gluttony, strong religious beliefs, the acquisition of wealth, yet generosity with it, and a love of knowledge; and finally, the seventh or Saturn line, is symbolic of a certain gloominess of character, a talent for learning foreign languages, an interest in agriculture and mining, and a desire for solitude.

When the forehead creases are short, or fine and irregular, or otherwise badly formed, they signify some negative expression of the character traits or qualities associated with them. Thus a person with a faint or broken Mercury line, for example, while yet possessing a skill with words, may use his loquacity to denigrate others; he may even become a book critic. Weak lines also indicate poor health, anxiety, and poor concentration.

Cardano also said that if the forehead creases are wavy at their ends, it indicates long voyages by sea; if the creases turn down at their ends, long journeys by land; and if the creases turn up, travel through the air!

High-set, well-formed creases denote the attainment of one's goals at an early age; middle-set creases portend success in middle life; and low-set creases reveal that the palm is achieved later in life. It is usually better to have well-marked and unbroken creases placed on the lower half of the forehead than on the upper half. Early success, especially if it is considerable, is rarely handled well and may cast a shadow over the rest of the life.

Chapter Eight
THE EYEBROWS

'He who is born under the sign of Aries has two thick bumps at the base of his forehead, such as may be seen on the forehead of the rams in our folds. His eyebrows are well arched and often join in the centre to form the hieroglyph of the sign. His eyes are set rather wide apart. He has a proud bearing but his head is always slightly inclined, for he is always ready to charge forward.'

From *Alexander the God* by Maurice Druon.

The eyebrows, according to the Chinese, are one of the face's Five Vital Features, which alone testifies to their importance. Indeed, no face can be properly read without due consideration being paid to them.

The eyebrows form the border between the Upper Zone and the Middle Zone of the face, belonging neither wholly to one nor to the other, yet at the same time being part of both. This gives them a certain intangible quality, which is why they are difficult to interpret, especially to the untrained eye.

Biologists believe that the eyebrows evolved to stop the sweat of the forehead from running down into the eyes, hence they are utilitarian and protective. They should therefore be sufficiently long and thick to carry out this task, which immediately suggests that those with eyebrows that are too short or too thin are not only improperly made in this respect, but are also deficient in some degree with regard to those personal characteristics symbolized by the eyebrows. And likewise, the eyebrows should neither be too thick nor too close together—or, at worst, meet in the middle—whereby they form a barrier between the Upper Zone and the Middle Zone.

Such a barrier reveals that the mental qualities represented by the former zone are kept separate from the more human qualities of the latter, thereby betokening a lack of conscience. In fact thick eyebrows betray a strong ego. They symbolize the person who wants to get ahead and make his mark on the world, and who won't let anyone or anything stand in his way. This is why those who become leaders often have thick eyebrows.

Your eyebrows signify your emotional type and the degree of understanding that exists between your head and your heart. In this respect they show how well you get on with others, especially those who are close to you. They also serve as a guide, along with the ears and the forehead, to your intellectual ability. And where the future is concerned, your eyebrows symbolize your fate between the ages of 30 and 33.

Ideally, your eyebrows should be in balance with the rest of your face. Hence their size should be neither too over-powering nor too small. At best, they should form a gently curving arch above each eye, being thickest above the inner corner of the eye and becoming gradually thinner towards their far end. Their colour should be the same as your hair, as eyebrows that are darker or lighter than the hair's natural colour disrupt the harmony of the face. The eyebrow hairs themselves should lie along the axis of the eyebrows, pointing away from the face's mid-line. It is not a good sign if the hairs are bushy or of unequal length. And the eyebrows should be well-defined, not broken or patchy in appearance.

One pair of eyebrows approaching the ideal belonged to Joan

Figure 79: Joan Blondell — eye-brows approaching the ideal

Blondell (see Figure 79), the film actress and one-time wife of Dick Powell. The reader will notice that her eyebrows are longer than her eyes, a feature which suggests above-average intelligence, without being too long. They are somewhat darker in colour than her hair, which is a negative feature, although this is doubtless caused by her dyeing her hair blond, which was as popular in the 1930s as it is today.

Joan Blondell made her first film, *Sinners' Holiday*, with James Cagney in 1930 and quickly went on to become a star. She was divorced from Powell in 1945, and two years later married impresario Mike Todd.

The two famous faces portrayed in Figure 80 each show a number of interesting features, not the least being the contrast between their eyebrows. Muhammed Ali's eyebrows are full, yet by no means overpowering, whereas Frank Sinatra's small eyebrows are out of balance with the rest of his face.

Ali's eyebrows are well-defined and have the same dark colour as his hair. They are also long, exceeding the length of his eyes. And while not as curved as they should be, nor exact mirror images of one another (the left is somewhat thinner than the right), they are otherwise of a superior type. Such eyebrows reveal that Ali is brighter than his not particularly high and uncreased forehead and his low-set ears suggest, that he enjoys tolerably good relations with others, and that his early 30s were probably the best years of his life.

Frank Sinatra's eyebrows, however, are shorter than his eyes, straight instead of curved, and of a different colour than his hair. They indicate that he does not have very warm personal relationships and that he is therefore something of a lonely soul. And while his large, high-set ears and ample forehead bespeak a high IQ, the

Figure 80: Muhammed Ali and Frank Sinatra

shortness of his eyebrows means that such an estimate must necessarily be reduced. His eyebrows also reveal that he went through a very difficult period during his early 30s, which would have been one of the worst times of his life.

The reader may care to note that both men have unbalanced faces, as each of their three facial zones have a different height. Both have a long Lower Zone and a shorter Upper Zone, while the Middle Zone is the shortest of the three. Hence neither man is properly integrated in a psychical sense.

The illustration of Junzo Okudairo (see Figure 5) shows us an example of negatively-formed eyebrows. They are set on a different level, they do not equal or surpass the length of the eyes, they are of

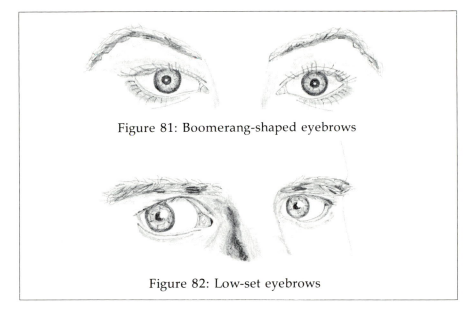

Figure 81: Boomerang-shaped eyebrows

Figure 82: Low-set eyebrows

uniform thickness, and they are bushy. In total, they suggest a disturbed and dangerous man.

When the eyebrows have the shape of a boomerang, rising to a central point instead of being curved (see Figure 81), they symbolize independence and strength of will, and thus the person who likes his own way and who wants to get ahead. These qualities are more pronounced if the angle of the inverted 'V' is sharper and higher. This shape was once called the 'Ruben's Point', after the artist who had similar eyebrows, and was believed to indicate an aptitude for mixing colours.

Eyebrows that are low-set, seeming to crush down upon the eyes (see Figure 82), are a negative sign, symbolizing an unnaturally prudent and calculative nature and a hesitant and insecure mind. Such a

Figure 83: High-set eyebrows

person's lack of flair and his dislike of taking a gamble means that he is more likely to achieve his goals late in life, if at all.

Very high-set eyebrows, contrarily, are symbolic of a devil-may-care, irresponsible attitude (see Figure 83), which while it may some-times result in early gains (but only if the ears and the forehead are well-shaped), often creates difficulties for, and brings heartache to, the person concerned.

Straight eyebrows are indicative of the practical, forthright and rather unimaginative person (see Figure 84a). This type likes to stick to the facts and get on with the job, yet he can be a problem if he is upset or asked to change course. Should straight eyebrows be broader at their outer ends (see Figure 84b), they betoken the man or woman who is stern, decisive, and a good leader, and who completes those projects he or she is asked to do. But such people make danger-ous enemies, because they will never rest until they have overcome those in opposition to them.

Eyebrows that slope upwards from the centre of the face, so giving their owner a devilish look (see Figure 85), signify a selfish and

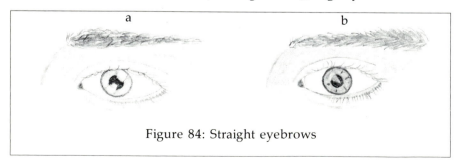

Figure 84: Straight eyebrows

egotistical person, the type who wants his own way and who believes that he is always right. He can go far in life when his confidence in himself is justified, but all too often he fails to deliver the goods and hurts others with his spite, anger, empty promises, and sheer pig-headedness.

When the eyebrows curve strongly downwards at their outer ends (see Figure 86), they betoken a shy and not very capable individual,

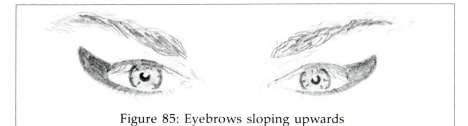

Figure 85: Eyebrows sloping upwards

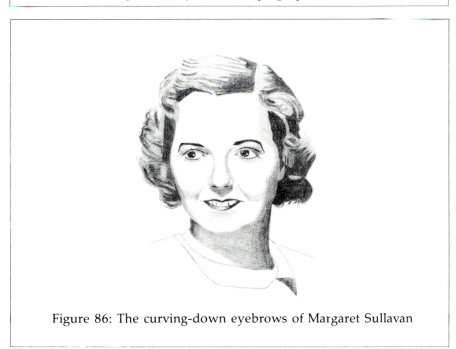

Figure 86: The curving-down eyebrows of Margaret Sullavan

whose fear of the world and lack of confidence make it very hard for him to get ahead.

These basic eyebrow shapes are modified in some degree by their thickness and by the direction of hair growth. Thick, bushy eyebrows (see Figure 87) betray the person who is irritable and aggressive; these unpleasant traits are worse if the hairs also grow in different directions. Cesare Lombroso noticed that the eyebrows of many criminals, notably rapists and murderers, are bushy.

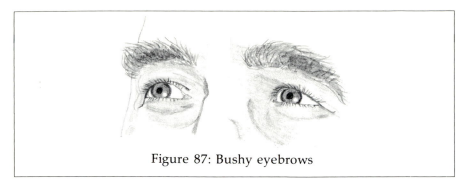

Figure 87: Bushy eyebrows

Eyebrow hairs that grow upwards (see Figure 88) signify a brave and resolute person, the sort who is always ready to accept a challenge. He will make his own way in the world and won't be discouraged by setbacks. Yet he finds it hard to live a quiet life as he quickly becomes bored.

When eyebrow hairs grow downwards they reveal a lack of energy and confidence, and hence the person who is faint-hearted. Such people easily get pushed aside and discouraged, which is why they often have to make do with the back seat in life.

Very thin eyebrows are one sign of a lack of inner sparkle and resolution, although such qualities will not be entirely absent if the brow itself is prominent. However, thin-eyebrowed people tend to drift through life without direction or purpose. Those who do find success are usually guided to it by a stronger Svengali-type, who manages their affairs.

It should always be borne in mind that many people, particularly women, pluck their eyebrows, which alters their natural shape and texture and so prevents them from being properly evaluated. Such modified eyebrows do not change the inner woman (or man); they only lie about her or him to the outside world.

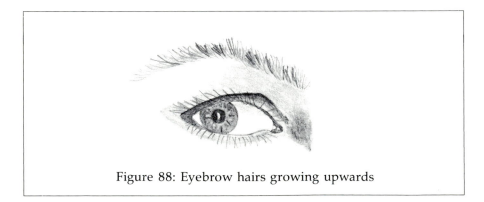

Figure 88: Eyebrow hairs growing upwards

Chapter Nine
THE EYES

'Round her eyes her tresses fell,
Which were blackest none could tell,
But long lashes veiled a light,
That had else been all too bright.'

From *Ruth* by Thomas Hood.

It has become a cliché to say that the eyes are the windows of the soul, but it is certainly true that by their shape, brightness and colour, and by the way that they move, the eyes provide a wealth of information about the inner person.

The eyes are of course sense organs, giving us the power of sight. Each eye is a spherical, fluid-filled capsule lodged within an orbit of the skull, and which can be rotated by the eye muscles. Light is admitted into it via a circular opening, the pupil, which appears at the front of the eye as a large black dot. The pupil is surrounded by a pigmented halo, the iris, that is coloured brown for most of the world's races, while for Europeans its colour varies from dark brown at one

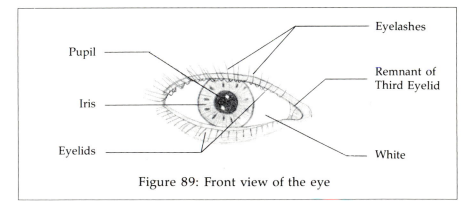

Pupil

Iris

Eyelids

Eyelashes

Remnant of
Third Eyelid

White

Figure 89: Front view of the eye

extreme to pale blue at the other. The visible remainder of the eye-ball front is known as the white and should ideally be this colour. The eyes can be closed and thus protected by the eyelids, whose short, projecting hairs, the lashes, assist in this capacity. The eye surface is kept moist by the tears, a special antiseptic fluid which brightens them (see Figure 89).

The eyes should be in balance with the rest of the face. They should therefore be neither too large nor too small, too bulging nor too sunken. They should be set on the same level, and they should also be horizontal, sloping neither upwards nor downwards. When the eyes are relaxed and looking forwards, the irises of both should be overlain somewhat at their top and bottom by the eyelids, so that there is no white showing either above or below them. The whites should likewise have no visible blood vessels in them, or be discoloured, or bear blotches. Eyes having all these positive features are symbolic of an honest, trustworthy, and confident person, who is likely to have a happy life and who will achieve many of his or her goals. They bespeak inner serenity, which is the fount of happiness.

However, the single most important eye feature is their shine or glitter. This unique, some would say magical, characteristic is produced by light interacting with the tears at the eye surface, and not only gives the eyes life but is also the measure of the interior sparkle of their owner. Bright, lively eyes belong to a bright and lively person, whereas dull, glitterless eyes are owned by someone who is not only tired and despondent, but also spiritually bankrupt. The difference between such eyes is illustrated by the two drawings below (see Figure 90). Princess Diana's eyes are glowingly alive, but Bo Derek's eyes are empty of life's spark.

Bright eyes, when they are combined with a direct and penetrating gaze, are said to be masterful. It is a look that belongs to those who

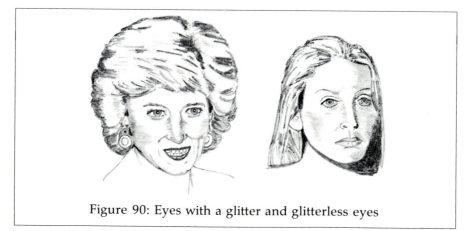

Figure 90: Eyes with a glitter and glitterless eyes

are destined to reach a position of power and authority. Those lacking masterful eyes cannot expect to reach the top positions, no matter how good their other facial features are.

Suetonius tells us that Julius Caesar had 'keen, dark brown eyes', and that his successor Augustus had eyes that were 'clear and bright, and he liked to believe that they shone with a sort of divine radiance: it gave him profound pleasure if anyone at whom he glanced keenly dropped his head as though dazzled by the sun'. And Plutarch records that Alexander the Great had a certain 'quickness of eye, in which many of his friends and successors most affected to imitate him'. The reader who wishes to observe the masterful eye in a modern leader has no better example than Margaret Thatcher, whose direct, brilliant and penetrating gaze could quieten an unruly pride of lions.

Bright eyes lacking a steady gaze are not masterful, but if their owners possess good, strong and balanced features, they may do well for themselves in such fields as the arts and entertainment, the civil service, and the groves of Academe. The seventeenth-century poet, playwright, and diplomat Sir John Denham was a man of this type. John Aubrey tells us that 'his eye was a kind of light goose-grey, not big; but it had a strange piercingness, not as to shining and glory, but (like a Momus) when he conversed with you he looked into your very thoughts'. He also notes that the philosopher Thomas Hobbes 'had a good eye, and that of a hazel colour, which was full of life and spirit, even to the last. When he was earnest in discourse, there shone (as it were) a bright live-coal within it'.

The less fortunate owners of bright eyes not only fail to control them properly, but have unbalanced yet strong facial features. They thus lack those necessary qualities of patience and perseverance, without which success is so hard to achieve, while possessing energy and a desire to make something of their lives. Their disappointments and failures give rise to frustration and anger, which both disrupts the harmony of their homes and causes them to suffer from ulcers and other stress-related disorders.

Those with bright eyes who cannot control their gaze and who have weak and unbalanced features, seldom advance themselves very far in life. Their energy is either undirected or expended on the wrong things, so earning them the contempt and indifference of others, although they are often quite happy with what they accomplish.

The eyes portend our fate between ages 34 and 39. Hence if your eyes are bright and steady, and show those other positive features mentioned in the third paragraph of this chapter, then this period will be (or was!) fortunate for you. You can expect to be happy and healthy, and to make advances in your work or career.

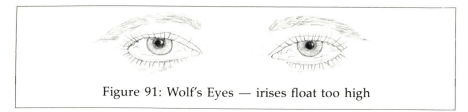

Figure 91: Wolf's Eyes — irises float too high

But if your eyes display one or more negative traits the period will not be so favourable. Yellowish-coloured whites or a blotch appearing in them, for example, presage a health breakdown and its attendant anxiety. The Chinese also claim that a blotch in the white of the eye betokens foolishness with money and the likelihood of its complete loss. The presence of blood vessels in the eye white is also a bad sign. They symbolize mental disquiet, a disturbed thought pattern, and possibly a violent disposition.

Irises that float too high revealing the white beneath them (see Figure 91) are evidence of an unstable, negative, and spiritually disturbed inner state, that of the person who is likely to be both a danger to himself and to others. Such people need very careful handling and should not be trusted. This is why eyes of this type are called Wolf's Eyes by the Chinese (see also Figure 91b).

The young model featured in Figure 91 is doubly unfortunate to have not only floating irises, but also visible blood vessels in her eye

Figure 91b: *Left* William Powell

Figure 92: Adolf Hitler

whites and eyebrows that are too low-set. These features reveal that she is dreadfully muddled and unhappy, and presage that she is likely to encounter major problems of one sort or another in her 30s.

It has sometimes been said that Adolf Hitler did not have the face of a madman or a criminal, but the perceptive reader should have no trouble in spotting some very negative features in the drawing shown opposite (see Figure 92).

However Hitler had, in one sense, very remarkable blue eyes, which shone with an almost hypnotic gleam, a fact remarked upon by many who met him. But this should not surprise us, as he became the German leader and was thus possessed of those inner strengths which enabled him to attain so eminent a position. Yet while his eyes had a masterful quality, their irises floated far too high, revealing the whites beneath them. This fact alone betrays Hitler's inner turmoil and unbalanced emotions, which were to find their perverse expression in the doctrines of the Nazi Party.

Floating irises also represent a difficult life period between ages 34 and 39. Adolf Hitler was born in 1889 and reached the age of 34 in 1923, the year in which he impetuously led the fledgling Nazi Party on a revolutionary 'march on Berlin', which was broken up by the police, who shot several of his followers and arrested him. Hitler was sent to prison for nine months, although he used the time profitably to write *Mein Kampf*, which became the Nazi bible. In fact the five years following 1923 were difficult for both Hitler and the Nazi Party, the latter being one of several competing political parties in the German democratic state, and they suffered a stunning defeat in the election of 1928, when Hitler was 39 years old. But the next few years were much kinder to the Nazis. They won large electoral gains in 1930, which they further increased in 1932. The following year Hitler eliminated his rivals in the party, and he won an outright election victory in 1934, at age 45, when he became Dictator. These later years are symbolized in Hitler's face by his nose, his best facial feature, when he reached the pinnacle of his success.

The irises can sometimes also sink too low, so that the white of the eye appears above them (see Figure 93). This is a rare but very negative eye form. It betokens a cruel and perverse nature, which belongs to the person who takes delight in causing suffering and distress. Those with this type of eye, like the preceding one, are likely to die comparatively young and often violently, but should they live to an advanced age, it will be lonely and unhappy.

More common are eyes that protrude to such an extent that the whites are visible both above and below the irises (see Figure 94). This condition, known medically as exophthalmos, is one of the symptoms of hyperthyroidism or over-activity of the thyroid gland,

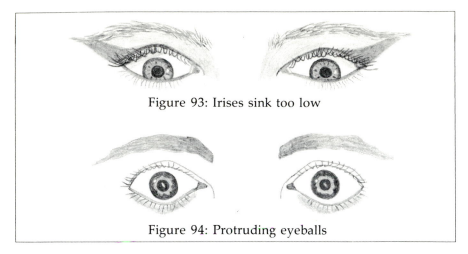

Figure 93: Irises sink too low

Figure 94: Protruding eyeballs

which produces a nervous and excitable state of mind, with an accompanying violence of temper and behaviour.

A similar, although less marked, temperamental and behaviour pattern occurs in those who have protruding eyes, but who are not suffering from any endocrinal malfunction. Such people typically express their anger as sarcasm. They are also both lascivious and jealous, and hence are likely to both cheat on their partners and to accuse them of infidelity. Thus it is not surprising that they often have a lonely and distressed old age.

Eyes that are one eye-length apart symbolize a good balance of the qualities represented by the eyes. When their spacing is wider, it reveals a reduction of mental quickness and agility, which is proportional to their distance apart. Hence when the eyes are very wide apart it suggests an impaired mind, even stupidity.

Eyes that are closer together than one eye-length are a sign of narrow views and a suspicious nature. Their owners lack warmth and tend to put their own needs and concerns first, which is why they cannot be trusted and why they have few close friends.

If your eyes are large, yet not so large as to disrupt the balance of your face, you are bold and adventurous, responsible and commanding. Indeed, those who occupy high positions in industry, commerce and politics often have large eyes. You may also possess above-average artistic talents.

Conversely, if your eyes are small, you are a less outgoing and a more cautious type, who prefers thinking to doing. You would rather work on your own than with others, and you enjoy tasks that are something of a challenge. You could make an excellent researcher, analyst or theorist, although your natural stubbornness will sometimes prevent you from exploring different and more productive paths. However, small-eyed women tend to be shrewish and demanding, while at the same time showing great loyalty to their husbands and families.

The colour of the eyes is imparted to them by a pigment named melanin. The more melanin that is present in the iris, the darker and browner the eye, while progressively less melanin results in lighter colours such as grey, green and blue. When there is no melanin in the irises at all, a condition which occurs in albinos, they are pink.

Brown eyes are traditionally associated with such personal qualities as warmth, openness, extroversion and excitability. Yet some caution is required before reaching this conclusion as by no means all brown-eyed people—who form the vast bulk of the human race—have these qualities. Hence while brown eyes suggest their presence, they must be judged or evaluated with regard to the rest of the face. It is true, however, that people with brown eyes are less sensitive to pain than are those with eyes of a lighter colour.

Hazel eyes are also indicative of warmth, yet this is admixed with greater intellectual vigour than that possessed on average by the brown-eyed. Aubrey tells us that the philosopher Thomas Hobbes 'had a good eye, and that of a hazel colour', and that Francis Bacon 'had a delicate, lively hazel eye'. Hazel-eyed people are less excitable than their brown-eyed compatriots, which enables them to cope better with the unexpected.

Blue eyes vary in tone from deep sapphire, through azure and aqua-marine, to the washed-out paleness common amongst American film-stars. The maxim with blue eyes is: the lighter the colour, the less passion and compassion. In general, blue eyes signify a calmer, quieter and more introverted personality than that of the brown-eyed, which implies rather conservative values and a liking for things the way they are. But those with dark blue eyes have more heat in them than their pale blue-eyed cousins, who are very cool and calculating. And while blue eyes of a darker hue belong to naturally peaceful people, it is a sad fact that rapists and murderers often have pale blue eyes. James Hanratty, the A6 murderer, was distinguished by his 'pale blue, staring eyes', as was Adolf Hitler. And we know from Suetonius that Nero, the insane Roman emperor who played his fiddle while Rome burned, had 'dullish blue' eyes.

Green eyes have received a good press over the years, although I have known so few people with eyes of this colour, that I cannot vouch for the truth of any of it. The green-eyed are reputed to be courageous and daring individualists, who are impishly cheerful, clever, and inventive, but this sounds like Irish blarney to me.

Grey eyes are possessed by those who are emotionally controlled, who need to think long and hard before committing themselves to

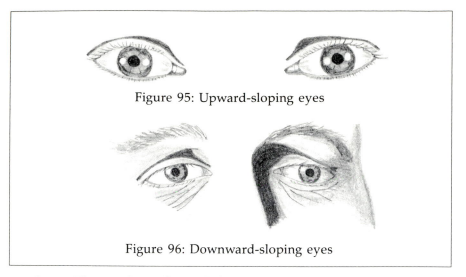

Figure 95: Upward-sloping eyes

Figure 96: Downward-sloping eyes

anything. The reader will recall that the virgin goddess Athene, who sprang fully armed from the head of Zeus, had grey eyes that 'did sparkle like the skies'. 'His eyes are a kind of goose-grey,' wrote John Aubrey of Sir William Petty, the surveyor and political economist, while Erasmus observed that Sir Thomas More, the celebrated author of *Utopia*, had 'eyes, bluish grey, with flecks here and there . . . His expression corresponds to his character, always shewing a pleasant and friendly gaiety, and rather set in a smiling look'.

The eyes should ideally lie horizontally, when they add to the balance of the face, although it is not a negative sign if they slope either upwards or downwards, unless the other facial features show some defect, when the qualities they signify may be used for bad purposes. And clearly, among Oriental people whose eyes normally slant upwards, it is only those with eyes that show a pronounced slant that have the personal characteristics mentioned below.

Eyes that slope upwards (see Figure 95) are the mark of the proud, self-important person, who believes that the world is his oyster and who wants to make the most of whatever opportunities come his way. He is outgoing, energetic, and ever ready to take risks. It is easy to imagine how such a person, given the opportunity, might be tempted into wrongdoing or crime.

Downward-sloping eyes (see Figure 96) have a doleful look, yet those with them are by no means sad or uncertain. Indeed, such eyes signify decency, generosity, and good-naturedness, and thus the person whose biggest fault is his readiness to believe the 'hard-luck' stories of those who would take advantage of him. This type has a constant heart and usually enjoys a stable and long-lasting marriage.

The creases or wrinkles that spread out from the corners of the eyes are known as 'crow's feet'. They are normally associated with old age, and indeed it is most unusual to meet an old person without them. But while up to four creases per eye can be regarded as a normal geriatric development, a larger number of creases is a negative sign, one suggestive of loneliness and personal difficulties.

Yet crow's feet are more revealing if they appear on the face of someone younger than 40, when they can be read as significators of character and fate. The presence of many such lines symbolizes indolence and a lack of purpose. Such a person makes a poor marriage partner, hence marital discord and divorce are likely, which will in turn bring unhappiness to the children of the union. Crow's feet that are long enough to reach to the temples reveal a lascivious nature and also a desire to make money without having to work for it.

When four or fewer creases form the crow's feet of a young person, it is important to note their direction of growth. An upward curve to the creases (see Figure 97) is very auspicious, and signifies good luck and a fortunate life, including a happy marriage.

Creases that curve downwards, on the other hand, have an unfortunate meaning (see Figure 98). They presage work and business difficulties, financial problems, and an unhappy marriage.

When one or more of the creases grow upwards and the remainder downwards, so that they cross like scissors (see Figure 99), they denote an argumentative disposition and an associated unwillingness to take advice. They are also the mark of a complainer. These character traits cause trouble for the person concerned, particularly in his close relationships.

Cesare Lombroso noted that born criminals often have upper eyelids that droop down at their centre, so giving their owner a sleepy appearance. This accords with what the Chinese say about such people, who they maintain are self-seeking, cunning, and unfeeling. When the whole of the upper eyelids droop, forming what is known as 'bedroom eyes', it signifies, as might be expected, lasciviousness and a preoccupation with seduction and affairs of the heart.

If a man's lower eyelids droop so as to expose their red inner borders, he is impotent; but should the owner of such eyelids be a woman, she is torrid and lustful.

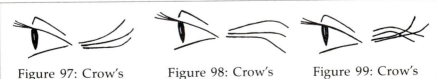

Figure 97: Crow's feet grow upwards

Figure 98: Crow's feet grow downwards

Figure 99: Crow's feet cross like scissors

Chapter Ten
THE NOSE

'His mind is concrete and fastidious,
His nose is remarkably big;
His visage is more or less hideous,
His beard it resembles a wig.'

From *How Pleasant to Know Mr. Lear* by Edward Lear.

The nose, jocularly known as the proboscis, stands in the middle portion of the Middle Zone of the face and thus occupies that most important of all Chinese placements, centre, where the palace of the Emperor was sited in ancient times, and where stands, in the sky above, the Pole Star. Centre is the 'direction' from whence everything flows, and to where all eventually returns. This is why astrologers place the nose under the rulership of Scorpio, for Scorpio also rules the sexual parts, which generate us all, and give Mars lordship of the right nostril and Venus that of the left. In myth, Venus was the goddess of love, and Mars was her paramour. But the connection between the nose and the sexual organs is closer than mere astrological tradition might suggest. Large noses have long been associated, at least in men, with larger than normal private parts, while small noses betoken the undersized. Indeed, Edward Lear, who is quoted above, is telling us more about himself than is often realized when he boasted that 'his nose is remarkably big'.

The importance of the nose as the fount of the face was recognized by Aristotle, and has been confirmed by virtually every later physiognomist of note. 'Of all the features of the human face,' wrote Dr Roger Rogerson, 'the nasal organ, being the most prominent, stands supreme as a revealer of character.'

We have already established that the height of the nose, or Middle Zone, should equal that of the forehead and of the lower third of the face. Such equal division of the face symbolizes inner balance, and thus those qualities like honesty, loyalty, and truthfulness, that are the hallmark of the good man and woman. Those with such balanced noses have a healthy sex drive, an optimistic outlook, and a sound view of themselves and their abilities. Yet these traits are only fully developed if the nose is well-shaped and if the other features are properly formed.

A long nose, that is, one whose length is greater than the height of the forehead or the Lower Zone, signifies a less open temperament and a stiffer demeanour. In fact the long-nosed tend to be rather snobbish and unduly proud of their accomplishments, yet scornful of those who wish to improve themselves. But the length of the nose must be set against its width. A broad nose, for instance, is indicative of stability and fixity of purpose, while a narrow nose symbolizes a more flighty and uncertain disposition. Hence the long and narrow nose belongs to the dilettante, who is often witty and engaging, but who consists of more shadow than substance, whereas the long and broad-nosed type is imbued with better concentration and far greater staying power, qualities that help him to find success. However, such breadth should be concentrated in the lower half of the nose, always providing that it is in balance with the rest of the face, and not at the top, where it portends, as we have already noted, an early death. Noses that are very long belong to men and women of noble character, and indeed to those who, like the nineteenth-century cleric Bishop Ken, are spiritually inclined (see Figure 100).

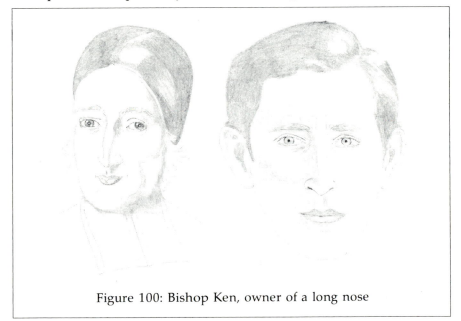

Figure 100: Bishop Ken, owner of a long nose

Short noses, such as are illustrated in Figure 80, not only deprive the face of balance, but symbolize a freer, less responsible, and somewhat untrustworthy type of person, who enjoys having a good time. Such people tend to be promiscuous, and do not mind bending the rules when necessary. But again, a wider nose represents greater emotional anchorage than a thin one, and thus signifies a more stable person.

The ideal nose, apart from having a height equal to that of both the forehead and the lower facial zone, has a straight bridge that does not bend to one side or to the other; a rounded, fleshy tip; well-shaped, flared wings; and nostrils that cannot be seen when the nose is viewed from the front. A near perfect nose was owned by the actress Norma Shearer (see Figure 101), although I'm not entirely certain that it was all of her own making.

This nose is popularly known as a Greek nose, although the types portrayed on Greek coins, apart from having a straight bridge, form a continuous or near continuous line with the forehead. Alexander the Great (see Figure 31) had a Greek nose—and no, he wasn't Greek, but Macedonian—as did Elvis Presley (see Figure 69). Yet both Alexander's nose and Elvis's nose were flawed by being too broad at their tops, between the eyes, which signifies a premature death. Such an unnatural width can be clearly seen in the half-face view of the two men shown in Figure 102.

Figure 101: Norma Shearer — the ideal nose

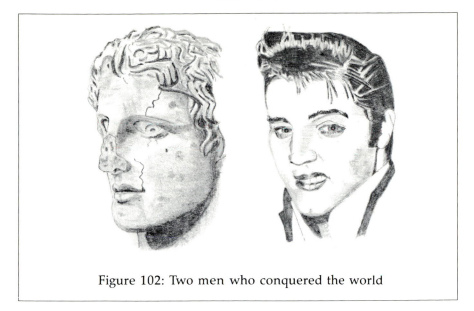

Figure 102: Two men who conquered the world

The Greek nose not only symbolizes a specific type of character, which includes a refined disposition, a love of art and music, and a natural authority, plus those positive traits mentioned earlier, but also portends, at best, a successful period of life between ages 40 and 49, which are the years covered by the nose.

However, such positive character traits and the likelihood of considerable mid-life success are weakened if two particular nasal angles are either too great or too small. One of these is the angle that the nose bridge makes, when viewed in profile, with the front of the face, the other is that subtended by the base of the nose (see Figure 103). The former should ideally measure about 30 degrees, and the latter

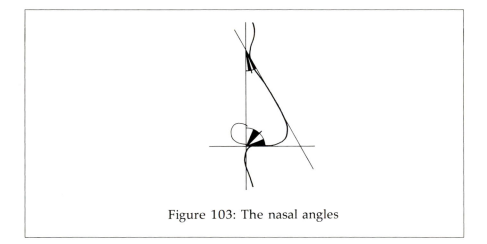

Figure 103: The nasal angles

about 90 degrees, which means, where the second is concerned, that the nostrils are not exposed when the face is observed from the front and that the nose does not bend down towards the mouth at its tip.

We find such ideal angularity in the profile of Alexander Pope (see Figure 50), and also in the drawing of the Reverend William Ellis (1795–1872), which is shown below, who devoted his life to missionary work in the South Seas and Madagascar (see Figure 104). In fact the reader may find it valuable to inspect not only the shape and angles of the Revd Ellis's nose, but also the other positive features of his face, and to judge these against what was said about him shortly after his death by a fellow churchman: 'God gave Mr Ellis a noble life—noble in its aims, spirit, actions, and results. His nobility and manliness could not but be marked. If there was anything he seemed truly to care for, it was holiness in the individual heart, and the growth of Christ's kingdom on earth.'

When the angle that the nose makes with the face approaches 40 degrees, or is greater, the nose has a sharp appearance (see Figure 105) , and thereby signifies a lessening of the positive qualities mentioned above and an accompanying temperamental shift towards excessive pride, irresponsibility, and curiosity, which is perhaps why this nose is commonly called the 'prod nose'.

Conversely, when the nose is flatter, so that the angle it makes with the face is less than 30 degrees, it betokens a lack of confidence. This

Figure 104: The Reverend William Ellis

type of person will not only need plenty of help and support if he is to get ahead, but may experience certain setbacks in his 40s.

A nose of whatever shape and angularity is affected by its fleshiness, which can improve a bad shape or spoil a nose that is well-formed. The best nose has a good covering of tissue, lacks sharp angles, has a rounded tip, and a decent width. Plumpness and roundness add fortune to the meaning of the nose, signifying as they do a warmth of manner and an optimistic outlook, a good income, and very often a skill in business. Very few people with thin, hard noses become rich or lead happy lives. Hence a nose that lacks flesh is a negative facial feature. It suggests a cold, anxious, and pessimistic nature, and an indifferent fortune.

When the nose turns up at its end so that the nostrils are visible from the front, forming what is known as a 'snub' nose, such an uplift signifies the happy-go-lucky and somewhat irresponsible person, who has difficulty in saving money and in making ends meet. These personal characteristics are heightened if the angle of tilt is great, as they are if the nostrils are large in size. Indeed, large exposed nostrils belong to those with loose morals, an aversion to work, and a love of gambling. Hence the Italian proverb, 'A turned up nose is worse than hail.'

A nose whose tip turns down towards the mouth belongs to a strongly-sexed person, whose needs in this respect are insistent and

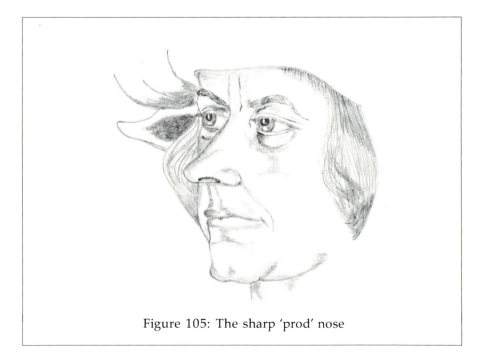

Figure 105: The sharp 'prod' nose

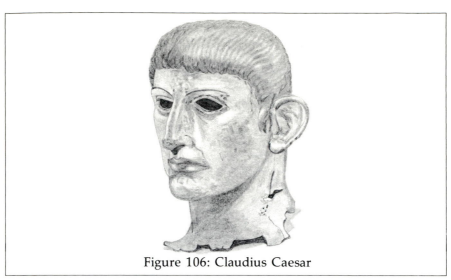

Figure 106: Claudius Caesar

demanding. He or she is also selfish, close with money, and untrustworthy. Yet the degree to which these negative traits occur is directly proportional to the amount of downward slope, and also the amount of 'body' that the nose has. And a moderate downward bend, such as affected the nose of Claudius Caesar (see Figure 106), may be positive when we consider the harm that such a man might have done had not his natural caution and dislike of excess stayed his hand. However 'his feelings for women were extremely passionate,' records Suetonius, adding, 'but boys and men left him cold'. In fact Claudius married four times. He divorced his first two wives, but was oblige to execute the third, Valeria Messalina, a nymphomaniac who injudiciously and bigamously married one of her lovers.

The reader should take special note of Claudius' outstanding ears, a facial feature that invariably signifies a troubled childhood, his low

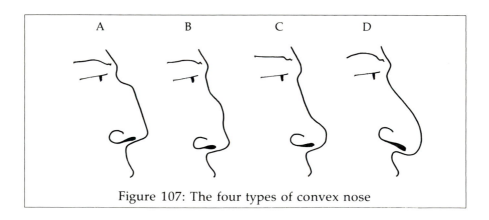

Figure 107: The four types of convex nose

forehead (notwithstanding his brushed-forward hair) and his thin eyebrows, and reflect upon the fact that his father Drusus died while on a campaign some months before he was born, that 'nearly the whole of his childhood and youth was so troubled by various diseases that he grew up dull-witted and had little physical strength', and that his mother often derided him as 'a monster: a man whom Mother Nature had begun to work upon but then flung aside'. It is also relevant to our study to point out that Claudius received the purple at age 50, which is the age symbolized by his clearly-marked philtrum, and that the following years, during which he both successfully governed Rome and conquered Britain, are represented by his well-shaped mouth and strong chin. Claudius died on 13 October, 54 AD, in his 64th year. He was apparently poisoned.

Claudius' nose is essentially of the Greek type, yet its bridge does have a slight outward bulge at its centre. This convexity of the bridge is often greater, and when it is the nose takes on a different form. Conversely, the bridge sometimes dips inwards towards the face, so producing a nose of the concave type.

There are four variants of the convex nose (see Figure 107). These are (a) the classic Roman nose, which has an upper convexity; (b) the nose, like that of Claudius, with a middle convexity; (c) the nose with a lower convexity, or bulge at its tip; and (d) the nose with a uniform convexity affecting its whole length, which is known familiarly as the hawk or Jewish nose.

The Roman nose is created by the prominence of the nasal bone, which juts out like a ledge and from which hangs the cartilaginous portion of the nose. This gives the nose a strong resemblance to the beak of an eagle, thus accounting for its description as 'aquiline' (from *aquila*, the Latin for 'eagle'). Such a nose symbolizes great energy, self-confidence, and firmness, and also a shrewd mind. It is the nose, in other words, of attack, which accounts for the fact that many famous leaders and military figures have this type of nose. The historian Suetonius tells us, perhaps not surprisingly, that the Emperor Augustus had 'a Roman nose', as did Sir Francis Drake, the Duke of Wellington, George Washington, Henry VII, Fernando Cortez, and Queen Elizabeth I. 'She was of person, tall,' wrote Thomas Fuller of the latter monarch; 'of hair and complexion, fair, well-favoured, but high-nosed.'

When the nose shows some degree of roundness at its middle, this convexity betokens a concern for the rights and privileges of others. The owner of this nose has energy and shrewdness like that of his Roman-nosed cousin, but he uses these, not to dominate and control, but to help and protect those less able than himself. Hence instead of being a nose of attack, it is one of defence. Let us take Claudius as but one example of a man with this nose type. We read that he was:

'a most conscientious judge: sitting in court even on his own birthday and those of his family, sometimes actually on ancient popular holidays or days of ill-omen. Instead of always observing the letter of the law, he let himself be guided by his sense of equity, and when he thought the punishments prescribed were either too lenient or too severe, he changed them accordingly'.

The nose with a lower bulge or convexity belongs to the person who expends his energy on making sure that his own needs are satisfied. It is thus the nose of both attack and defence, but always with the self in mind. Those who stand in its owner's way are beaten down, while those who laugh at or condemn his vanity and ambition are resisted. This explains why many actors and entertainers have such a nose, for they have to fight hard to get themselves in the spotlight. A modest example of this nose type was possessed by the film actress Rochelle Hudson, whose profile is shown in Figure 108. It is interesting to observe that her nose is also somewhat uptilted, thereby partially exposing her nostrils to view, a feature which reveals she was both light-hearted and irresponsible, characteristics that perhaps prevented her from becoming a major star.

Lastly, the hawk or Jewish nose, which is curved outwards from top to bottom, has long associations with financial expertise and business acumen, shrewdness and energy. This is indeed true, yet such traits and noses are by no means possessed only by Jews. Prominent businessmen the world over have convex noses, of whom the late Aristotle Onassis is but one example. But we must distinguish between a thin convex nose and one that is plump and fleshy. The former belongs to the person who, while energetic, lacks staying power. He is prepared to gamble and take risks, which may sometimes pay off but which frequently lead him into debt, and have him breaking agreements, reneging on promises, and falling out with those who have helped or backed him. This type all too often leads a lonely and uncertain life, treading as he does a narrow path between legality and illegality, and only enjoying temporary periods of affluence if he is lucky. The true Jewish nose, on the other hand, is plump and well-rounded. It symbolizes a temperament that is both energetic and stable, and optimistic and ambitious, characteristics that are the necessary precursors of success in any field.

A concave nose lacks the cartilage, and sometimes the bone, that gives the previously discussed noses their body, and often has a broad, flattened appearance, as if it had been struck by a fist. Such noses invariably subtend an angle of less than 30 degrees to the face, which is evidence of character weakness, and are typically accompanied by upturned nostrils, the true snub nose. But when the nose is not upturned it is termed 'Celestial', so-called because it was once thought to enhance a woman's beauty, not only by its shape but from its associated ideal feminine qualities of chastity and obedience. In fact concave noses have long been known to signify passivity, cowardice, weakness of will, and lack of energy. These characteristics find their most negative expression in the snub-nosed, when they are allied with loose morals and irresponsibility, which necessarily worsens them, in the same way that sewage added to a stagnant pool renders something unpleasant both noxious and dangerous. Indeed, Cesare Lombroso observed that many criminals have concave snub-noses.

The nose forms part of the face's mid-line, which should be straight. It is a negative sign if the nose is either tilted or twisted, or if it is bent to one side. The same is true if the nose is asymmetrical, one half being of a different shape to the other. Such lack of balance weakens whatever positive features the nose may have, and gives an evil cast to the meaning of its negative features. An imbalanced nose also portends a troubled and unhappy life period between the ages of 40 and 49.

'But what about me?' I hear you cry. 'My nose was perfectly straight until it was broken in a fight/car accident/game of rugby! Will such a rearrangement of my features alter my character and worsen my fate?'

I regret to say that it will, and this applies to any injury that causes permanent damage to the face. And it is not too difficult to under-

Figure 108: Rochelle Hudson

Figure 109: Albert Victor, the Duke of Clarence (1864–1892), and grandson of Queen Victoria. Once suspected of being Jack the Ripper.

stand why this should be. For if a person who once presented a fine Greek nose to the world has it flattened in a bout of fisticuffs, he not only feels different about himself, which in turn brings about a gradual change in his character, but is also responded to in a different way by others, which affects his relationships and may thus change his fate. This stems from the fact that the most important events of our lives often turn upon small, chance happenings. For example, a man with a newly-flattened nose may be ignored by the girl at a dance who would previously have found him attractive, and who may have later dated him, married him, and made him a wonderful wife, while another girl is lured by his bruiser-like looks, and chats him up, walks out with him, and finally makes an honest man of him. Yet if this marriage ends in a mid-life divorce, separates him from his children, drives him to drink, robs him of his self-respect, and eventually loses him his job, then we can appreciate how so minor an injury—a broken nose—completely altered his life and fortune.

Sometimes the nose, when viewed from the front, is noticeably thicker in the middle (see Figure 109). This is another negative feature, especially for a woman as it signifies the loss of her husband, by either divorce or death, in her 40s, and may mean, unless the lower part of her face is well-formed, a lonely old age. And both men and women with this type of nose usually have to work very hard, but often don't get the rewards they deserve. This is partly their own fault as they are very stubborn and thus reluctant to change course when they should.

Just as hair growing from the ear-holes is a bad sign, so too is hair growing from the nostrils. Indeed, a hairy nose is the mark of a gambler, the person who takes too many risks and who ultimately loses everything. It is never wise to go into business with or loan money to a person with a hairy nose.

The shape and size of your nostrils say a lot about your character. If your nose has flattened wings, for example, which result in narrow nostrils, you have a poor money sense. You not only find it hard to acquire money, but you rarely use it sensibly either.

In general, large nostrils belong to the financially careless, who let money slip through their fingers, whereas small nostrils are owned by those who are careful with money and who opt for a steady, secure job, rather than one which involves taking risks.

If your nostrils are square in shape you have a conservative disposition: you think you know how the world should be run, and you don't easily change your mind about anything. Others find you thick-skinned and thick-headed.

Should your nostrils be triangular in shape you are basically a Silas Marner type: you like to hoard your money and keep a tight control on your expenditures. You will seldom, if ever, be in need, but neither will you get much enjoyment from your wealth.

You are a rather prissy and precise person if you have round nostrils. You like things done your way, and you like to tell others what to do and how to behave. However, your ideas can sometimes be fresh and interesting, which prevents you from being a crashing bore.

If you have rectangular or elliptical nostrils whose long axis lies parallel to the septum of your nose, then you are an outgoing and adventurous type, who enjoys taking the occasional risk and having a bit of fun, although you do find it hard to save. In this respect you are quite different from the person who has similarly-shaped nostrils whose long axis lies parallel to the face. Such people tend to be dull, self-satisfied, and uninterested in anything new. But because they are self-indulgent and weak-willed, they have trouble saving their money.

A nose that is too small robs the face of balance and symbolizes a deficient character and an unfortunate fate. The small-nosed are emotionally unstable, have a weak libido, and are dishonest, traits which adversely affect their relationships, notably with those to whom they are closest. A small nose is also one sign of a short life.

The nose, however, must also be considered from the point of view of its colour, visible veins, creases, and skin defects. A bad colour or the presence of certain markings can rob even a well-shaped nose of much, if not all, of its positive significance. Hence these factors should be carefully considered.

Ideally, the nose should not have a colour that is darker or lighter, or markedly different, from that of the rest of the face, always providing that the general coloration is normal. This means that the nose of a European should be pink or light red in colour and have a radiant, healthy glow. If the nose itself has a good shape and size, such a colour and tone presages good health, a sound psyche, wealth, success, and recognition.

A nose that is red in colour, especially a dark red, portends financial difficulties, disagreements with relatives and friends, poor health and a short life. 'He was of middle stature and slight strength, brisk round eye, reddish-faced and a red nose (ill liver),' wrote John Aubrey of Sir John Suckling, the poet and courtier, who committed suicide at age 33. Hence it is ironic, considering the knight's flushed complexion, that his most famous poem should begin:

'Why so pale and wan, fond lover?
Prithee, why so pale?
Will, when looking well can't move her,
Looking ill prevail?
Prithee, why so pale?'

A red nose is often the result of an over-indulgence in strong drink, which in itself can bring about the problems mentioned above. Indeed, the red-nosed are frequently licentious and irresponsible.

A nose that is yellowish-pink in colour is generally fortunate. Its owner is lucky and has a lot of success.

A nose that is very dark in colour, so that it is bluish or blackish in appearance, is rarely seen, which is fortunate as it presages serious problems for its owner, in the shape of either illness, imprisonment, or financial disaster.

When deep creases run across the nose bridge of a man they warn of a bad accident, which may result in his death. In a woman such creases portend an unhappy marriage, which ends in divorce. If the creases are vertical they indicate that the person concerned will be childless, possibly as a result of infertility.

Skin defects like a rash, or blackheads, or whiteheads, when permanently present on the nose, betoken a reduced libido and possible impotence or frigidity during the middle years. And visible veins on the nose belong to a promiscuous person with low moral standards.

Chapter Eleven
THE MOUTH

'The music swells. His gross legs quiver.
His little lips are bright with slime.'

From *Wagner* by Rupert Brooke.

The mouth, being the outer opening of our hinged jaws, is the most mobile part of the face, a portcullis that admits food, drink, and air, which sustain us; that bites, when necessary, to defend us; and that speaks our thoughts, laughs our joy and mirth, and kisses those whom we love. Hence it is hardly surprising that the mouth's shape and form say much about us, and we must examine its variety of types with care. We shall be most concerned with the size of the mouth and the shape of the lips, although some attention will also be given to the teeth and the tongue which, while hidden from view to a large extent, contribute to the meaning of the mouth.

A bad mouth, in the sense of it being unlovely in appearance, does not necessarily mean that its owner has a reprehensible character or that he will fail to reach high office, but it does presage trouble for him during the years which it covers, these being from ages 51 to 54, and age 59. The previously mentioned Claudius, for example, was unfortunate to have had 'several disagreeable traits—an uncontrollable laugh, slobbering at the mouth and running at the nose, a stammer, and a persistent tic', while King James I, who succeeded Good Queen Bess, possessed 'a tongue too large for his mouth, which ever made him speak full in the mouth, and made him drink very uncomely, as if eating his drink, which came out into the cup of each side of his mouth . . . (yet) he was very witty and had as many witty jests as any man living, at which he would not smile himself, but deliver them in a grave and serious manner'.

The ideal mouth is of moderate size and has full, well-shaped lips

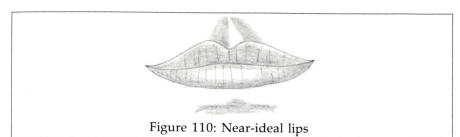

Figure 110: Near-ideal lips

that are of equal thickness and light red in colour. Each half of the
mouth is a mirror image of the other. The lips close together without
leaving a space between them, and they turn up at the corners. They
also have a natural radiance, yet are not made moist by saliva. A
man's lips should be firm, but not hard, and a woman's lips should be
soft, but not flabby (see Figure 110).

If you have such a mouth, then you have a warm, caring, honest
nature, a resolute character, and a fixity of purpose. It also reveals
that what success you gain in your 40s will lead to increased respect
and acclaim in your 50s.

A large mouth is one sign of an outgoing, extroverted, open, and
generous person. As such, these traits attract more attention and
bring greater popularity than that normally acquired by the owner of
a modest-sized mouth. But a large mouth also betrays a lack of any
clear purpose in life and a certain weakness of resolve, which often
means that its owner fails to capitalize on his social skills and whose
loud laughter and desire for company only earns him the scorn of
those who are going places. However, women with large mouths
tend to advance themselves more easily than large-mouthed men.
They do particularly well in the entertainment industry and in
business.

Small-mouthed people are both more introverted and more
careful and cautious than their large-mouthed cousins. Indeed, a
small mouth often signals a lack of confidence and an accompanying
suspicion of other people's motives and actions. Hence such types
tend to play their cards close to their chests. They either avoid company or endure it in order to find out what everybody else is up to.
And they hate spending money unnecessarily.

Thin lips signify a lack of both warmth and a genuine sympathy for
others, qualities that are directly proportional to the thinness of the
lips, and thereby suggest that their owner has few close relationships,
and that he will, particularly during his middle years, lead a lonely
life. Thin lips that fail to meet properly, or which are twisted or otherwise unbalanced, betoken a cruel and vengeful nature. A small
mouth with thin lips is the mark of a cold, closed and unfriendly

person, whose qualities derive from the inferiority complex characteristic of the type.

It is always a good sign when the lips are full and well-shaped, although they cannot be considered ideal unless they are also of equal size, turn up at the corners, and meet in a gently arched line (see Figure 110). Indeed, the size of your upper lip denotes your ability to love, while that of your lower lip reveals your need for love. The strength of these two qualities should be approximately the same, or else you will want more that you can give or vice versa. Hence when the upper lip is plumper than the lower, it signifies an ardent nature without the capacity to fully respond, while a larger lower lip bespeaks a great need for love but a reduced ability to love in return. The latter type thus tends to be disappointed in his expectations and is regarded as somewhat cool by those who fall in love with him (see Figure 111).

If your lips meet in a straight line, you have a careful, orderly, and calculating mind, which necessarily interferes with your emotional responses, sometimes to your detriment. Hence the lips shown overleaf (see Figure 112) belong to a woman who needs to be loved and who uses her brain to get what she wants, although she will doubtless never be wholly happy with any of her admirers or lovers.

When the line between the lips is straight but not exactly so in the middle (see Figure 113), it symbolizes the person, who, while being stable and somewhat uptight, has occasional urges to break free from his shell and behave audaciously, much to everyone's surprise. Hence such a mark betrays a certain impulsiveness of action.

Lips that meet in a gently curving line and which turn up at the

Figure 111: Fay Wray — a plumper lower lip

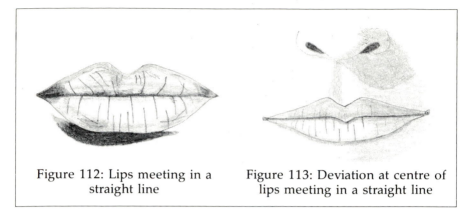

Figure 112: Lips meeting in a
straight line

Figure 113: Deviation at centre of
lips meeting in a straight line

corners belong to someone who is open and friendly, yet by no means unassertive (see Figure 114). In fact should the lips themselves be full, the person concerned is quite capable of holding down a responsible job and will direct and organize others in a fair and tactful manner. But because such lips also indicate a sensuous nature, the owner may unnecessarily complicate his life by becoming involved in extra-marital or otherwise risky love-affairs. This is particularly true of the person whose upper lip is plumper than the lower.

When the lips meet in an even, upwardly curving line and have a bright pink colour, they denote the person who is seldom lost for words and who has considerable powers of persuasion (see Figure 115). Such people are outgoing and quite creative, yet have a schem-

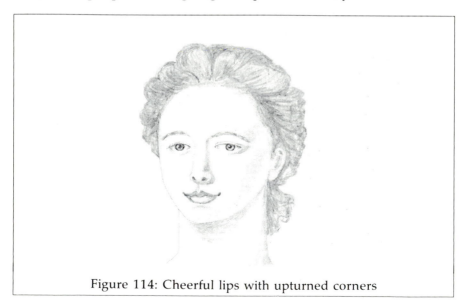

Figure 114: Cheerful lips with upturned corners

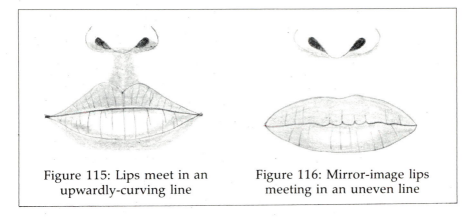

| Figure 115: Lips meet in an upwardly-curving line | Figure 116: Mirror-image lips meeting in an uneven line |

ing nature, which causes problems for them with others. However, a lip line of this type signifies a close family life and the acquisition of wealth.

Lips that meet in an uneven line betoken a somewhat troubled personality, and belong to the person who often feels misunderstood, and who, as a result, is unhappy. Such inner tensions are further emphasized in the lips shown in Figure 116, which have such a lip line, by the fact that the upper lip is almost a mirror image of the lower. The owner of this type of mouth has a strong sex urge, which encourages intimacy before emotional involvement and so brings about unwise and often unhappy encounters with the opposite sex.

Should lips of the latter type be further emphasized by their fullness, they symbolize a highly sensuous person who often behaves in

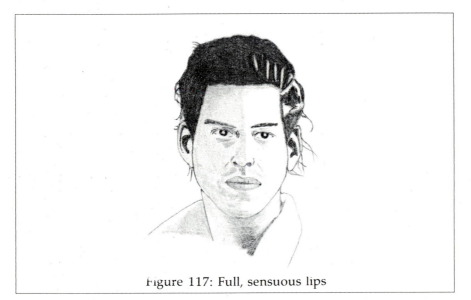

Figure 117: Full, sensuous lips

a dashingly romantic way, but whose chief concern is the gratifi-
cation of his, or her, sexual desires (see Figure 117). Such a person,
however, is blessed with a strong constitution and a healthy appetite.

Cesare Lombroso observed that the lips of rapists (and also those
of murderers) are frequently larger than average, having as they do a
fleshy, swollen appearance and protrude somewhat from the face.
Indeed, a protruding upper lip alone in a man reveals a strong sex
drive.

If the corners of thin, pale lips curve downwards, they form what
the Chinese call a 'fish's mouth' (see Figure 118). Lips of this type
belong to the irresolute, rather vague person, who brings trouble on
his head by speaking out of turn. When the lips are fuller, the will
power and strength of purpose are greater, which helps the person
concerned to behave more sensibly and confidently. Yet he will still
delight in gossip and in propagating scurrilous stories. Such an
individual often has a stormy marriage.

Lips with turned-down corners portend difficulties during their
owner's early 50s, when his or her marriage may fail or end with the
death of the spouse, and hence a lonely old age. If a downturned
mouth is accompanied by a weak chin and if the face lacks
cheeklines, the life will be short.

Teeth that are moderately long, regular, set close together, and
white in colour, are indicative of good fortune during the middle
years. The reverse is the case if the teeth are short, irregular, set apart
from one another, and discoloured, when they not only signify bad
luck but reveal that their owner is irresponsible, accident prone, and
has a poor financial sense. Indeed, teeth of this type, when found in
an unbalanced and weak face, betoken an unhappy life and an early
death. Short teeth by themselves indicate impatience and a difficulty
in saving money. Long teeth signify contrary qualities.

The smile is important when analysing the mouth. Those who
smile without parting their lips have something to hide and should
not be trusted.

A smile that reveals only the upper teeth, but not the upper gums,
is one sign of a good heart, an honest nature, and a pleasant fate,
although the teeth and lips must also be favourably fashioned to
make such an analysis certain. If the upper gums are also exposed by
the smile (see Figure 119), this reveals a depressive tendency that
can impair their owner's happiness and negatively affect his or her
career.

When both the upper and the lower teeth are exposed by the
smile, they signify a person of an open, fair, and generous character,
but who will suffer from the attacks and dislike of others. However,
women of low morals often have such smiles.

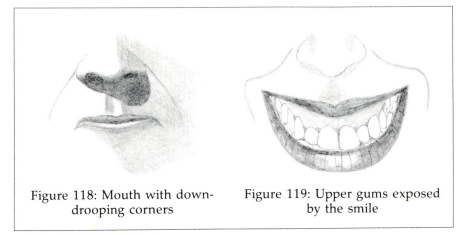

Figure 118: Mouth with down-drooping corners

Figure 119: Upper gums exposed by the smile

It is rare for the lower teeth only to be shown by the smile. Such unnaturalness betokens a stubborn and defensive nature, belonging to people who feel inferior but who refuse to let anyone grind them underfoot. They are radicals, but may, should they possess unbalanced features, be tempted into crime or revolutionary politics.

The tongue does not play a large part in face-reading because it is normally only intermittently visible, although it is a most important organ. It not only provides us with our sense of taste and enables us to properly masticate our food, but it on occasions permits us, by being extended between the teeth, to express our disapproval of those whom we consider to be nasty or asinine. King James I suffered throughout his life from the indignity of having too large a tongue, but this was infinitely better for his subjects than having a swollen head. 'In a word,' says our commentator Sir Anthony Weldon, 'he was such a King I wish this kingdom never had any worse, for he lived in peace, died in peace, and left all his kingdom in a peaceable condition, with his motto *Beati Pacifici.*'

But it must be noted that a large and broad tongue is lucky from a health and fortune point of view, and should its owner be able to touch the end of his own nose with it, he will become both wealthy and esteemed. A long, narrow tongue, by contrast, is unfortunate in meaning, for while it signifies verbal fluency, such a command of words is likely to be used at the expense of others. It also warns of bad luck, especially if the tip of the tongue cannot be applied to the end of the nose. Short tongues signify a greedy, critical nature and general misfortune.

However, each of these shapes benefit if the tongue is a dark pink colour, which improves their meaning, whereas tongues of other colours, such as grey, white, or bright red, betoken a lack of respect, indifferent health, and bad luck.

And lastly, regarding mouth odours, it is pertinent to take note of Aristotle's observation, that 'He whose mouth smells of a bad breath is one of a corrupted liver or lungs, is oftentimes vain, wanton, deceitful, of indifferent intellect, envious, covetous, and a promise breaker. He that has sweet breath, is the contrary.'

Chapter Twelve
THE CHIN, JAW, AND CHEEKBONES

'*Demolitiousness*: the propensity to mar, deface and destroy. The low, flat nose, which is particularly wide where the wings of the nostrils join the face; the wide, short ear . . . large neck, heavy jaws, and low forehead, are the signs which point out large destructiveness as unerringly as the shadow on the dial indicates the direction of the sun.'

From *Nature's Revelations of Character* by Joseph Simms.

No study of the form of the face is complete without some attention being given to the chin, the jaw, and the cheekbones, all of which may either corroborate or perhaps emphasize the character and fortune indications given by the other features, or show that they cannot be taken, if you'll excuse the expression, at face value. The best face has a strongly fashioned chin, jaw, and cheekbones, while any weakness in one or other of these areas undermines, to some degree at least, the rest of the face.

We all know what is meant by a 'weak' chin—one that is either too narrow, too pointed, or receding—and have no difficulty in distinguishing a 'strong' chin by its breadth and fullness. And neither are we wrong in our instinctive estimation of the meaning of such chins. Indeed, Cesare Lombroso noted that born criminals tend to have chins which are either small and receding, or which are excessively long, short, or flat, like those of apes. Chins of this type do not indicate criminality *per se*, but rather suggest a lack of drive and determination, which would otherwise be sufficient to keep the person concerned on the straight and narrow.

Hence your chin reveals the amount of will-power you have and also, like the lips, your capacity to, and your need for, love. It likewise betokens the quality of life that you can look forward to in your seventh decade (age 61–70).

Your chin, when viewed from the front, should ideally be broad,

Figure 120: The broad, round
chin of Barbara Stanwyk

Figure 121: The broad, square
chin of the pre-war dance band
leader Sydney Lipton

deep, and full. If it is, you have a strong character and considerable
determination, and you will also enjoy both good health and good
fortune in your 60s. And if your other features reveal that you gained
(or will gain) wealth and success in your early years, these will be
retained in your old age.

A broad, round chin is symbolic of generosity, emotional warmth,
ease-of-manner, and good humour, which are more readily and easily expressed if the chin is short. A deeper chin betokens an authoritarian streak, and thus typically belongs to the charming boss or exec-
utive who uses his warmth to win over, and so better control, his
employees and rivals (see Figure 120).

A broad, square chin is a mark of steadiness and trustworthiness,
qualities that enable the chin's owner to work hard and so do well in
both his career and marriage. The manner is less affable than that of
the person with the round chin, but the feelings are nonetheless deep
(see Figure 121). A square chin with a centrally-placed groove or
cleft shows a need to be loved. This explains why many artists and
entertainers often have chins of this type.

A broad chin which juts forward to some extent adds to its
strength and so emphasizes the positive qualities that are associated
with it. Yet this chin, when accompanied by a wide jaw, typically
signifies both a strong sex drive and an urge to seduce. Hence it is
not surprising to find that the late President John F. Kennedy, who
was an incorrigible womanizer, had a wide jaw and a jutting chin.

A narrow chin and a pointed chin both symbolize a weaker character, and less energy and drive, than that indicated by a broad chin; they also presage a troubled and perhaps lonely old age. However, if such chins are partnered by other weak facial features, they reveal that the life will be short.

A receding chin is very negative in meaning (see Figure 122), as it betokens a lack of self-esteem, indecision, uncertainty, and low energy, while at the same time forewarning that the later years may be made difficult by ill-health, poverty, and loneliness. Yet if a receding chin is broad it shows that, while its owner finds it hard to make decisions, once made he, or she, adheres to them with great obstinacy.

Because the chin is the front part of the jaw, it necessarily reflects the build of the jaw. Thus a broad chin invariably accompanies a wide jaw, and vice versa. And the jaw shape is determined by the shape of the face. When the face is square or rectangular, the jaw and chin are broad and square, and when it is round they are rounded. A face of the upright triangle type or the truncated upright triangle type, has a very wide jaw and a strong chin, while the face with the shape of an inverted triangle has a narrow jaw and a pointed chin. The face shape known as the amputated inverted triangle—the Venus face—has a jaw and a chin of intermediate width.

A wide jaw is one sign of great energy and strength of will, hence those with such a jaw tend to be very determined, resolute and ambitious; they also have, as we have previously remarked, a strong libido. Hence those with a narrower jaw have proportionally less of these qualities.

Yet the jaw must also be examined from the side before it can be properly evaluated. When the jaw-bone is deep below the ear (see Figure 123), it is another indication of a strong will-power. Should such a depth of jaw be allied with a great width of jaw, then the per-

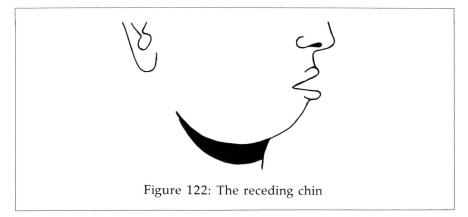

Figure 122: The receding chin

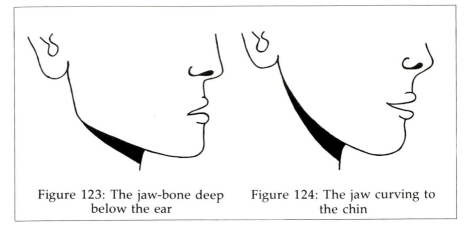

Figure 123: The jaw-bone deep   Figure 124: The jaw curving to
        below the ear   the chin

son concerned is very resolute and determined, which naturally helps him to achieve his ends. This is why those with rectangular faces, whose jaws are both wide and deep, so often become captains of industry and leaders of men.

In this respect it is interesting to note that Pericles, the ancient Greek statesman and orator, who led his fellow Athenians to victory over the other city-states, had a head that was disproportionally long, which led to certain poetic wags calling him *Schinocephalus* or 'Onion-head'—the onions they were referring to being the long sea onions, not the near-spherical types that we grow in our gardens.

A more moderate depth of jaw beneath the ear implies a less strong will-power, which reduces what might otherwise be obstinacy to manageable proportions.

It is more common, however, to find that the jaw, instead of descending in a straight line below the ear and then turning quite sharply to form the underside of the chin, proceeds in a gentle curve from the ear to the point of the chin (see Figure 124). If such a curvature is combined with a wide jaw, the two together suggest will-power tempered by flexibility, whereas if the jaw is also narrow, the will is weak and the determination non-existent.

The cheekbones are in reality the lower borders of the orbits or eye sockets, which widen (or deepen) as they progress from the nose. The cheekbones sometimes project sufficiently to be noticeable, or they may show no visible bulge at all. Their height also varies, high cheekbones crowding up against the eyes, while low cheekbones become lost in the tissue forming the cheeks. And again, the cheekbones may be well-covered by flesh, or at the other extreme, the skin may be drawn tightly over them. Each of these variations reveals another facet of character and fortune.

With regard to age, the cheekbones are linked with the mid-40s, the left to age 45, the right to age 46. If one or both cheekbones are badly formed or are damaged, or if they lie at different levels, so upsetting the balance of the face, then these years will be bad for their owner, who will doubtless suffer a fall from grace at this time or be robbed of some or all of the authority that he has achieved.

The cheekbones betoken the power of command and the degree of influence that you are likely to attain. If you have high, visible, and well-covered cheekbones, and if your other facial features are good, you will not only gain authority, but will use your power in a fair and noble way. Yet if your cheekbones are high and visible, but are bony, then you will use the power you achieve unfairly and ignobly, indeed possibly even cruelly. High, but flat cheekbones suggest authority without the power of command, and hence typically belong to those who become academically eminent, for example.

If your cheekbones are low-set, or if they are thin or weak in form, then you are unlikely to rise to any position of power or become at all influential. You must therefore expect to remain one of the unknown workers of the world.

The male face is naturally hirsute, although the fashion of the moment is for it to be shaved. Yet the colour, thickness, heaviness, and direction of hair growth of the beard can provide some useful information about the character and the fate of a man.

The beard grows on the sides of the face, the jaw, the chin, and the upper lip, and thus only refers, where the fate is concerned, to the years of a man's life that are associated with these parts, that is, from age 50 through to age 82, and also to the middle 90s (see Figure 43). The quality of the beard will either detract from, sustain, or enhance, the character and fortune indications of the areas which it covers.

The best and most positive type of beard has a full growth and a dark colour, and its hair is fine, soft, springy, and glistening. It does not grow closely around the mouth as if to seal it in, but shows some bare skin beneath the lower lip. It also grows in the philtrum or groove. Such a beard represents hard-working, honest, steady, and generous qualities, and thus augments the meaning of the lower part of the face. It likewise portends that the middle years and the old age of the man will be healthy, happy and successful.

But when a beard of full growth is formed of coarse, wiry, dull, and grizzled hair, which has a reddish or a yellowish colour, it spoils the meaning of the lower face, signifying that its owner's character is, or will become, uncouth and grasping, his temper angry and mean, and his life threatened by ill-health, injury, or violence. This negative interpretation is doubly applicable if such a beard grows closely around the mouth, which is always a sign of danger to the life in the middle years. We see this close growth of the beard about the mouth

Figure 125: Sir Francis Crossley

in Figure 125, which portrays the Victorian philanthropist Sir Francis Crossley, Bart.

Sir Francis, who was born in 1817 in Halifax, built up a highly-profitable trading business there with his two brothers, which was eventually to employ 5000 people, of whom many were made partners in the company. A man of strong religious principles, Sir Francis is still remembered in Halifax today for his construction of the People's Park, which was sited so as to be 'within the walk of every working-man in Halifax; that he shall go and take his stroll there after he has done his day's toil, and be able to get home again without being tired'. Yet as his beard presages, Sir Francis became ill in his 51st year. The sickness encouraged him to attempt a visit to the Holy Land, but he was forced by a worsening of his condition to break his journey at Rome, where he remained for many months. On his return to England he felt quite well for a period, but suffered a relapse toward the end of 1871, and died on 5 January 1872, aged 54.

A beard that grows thinly, or is patchy in appearance, symbolizes a weak character, a lack of energy and resolve, and a troubled later life, one blighted by poor health and an absence of success. And if the moustache does not grow in the philtrum, its owner will be unfairly criticized or slandered.

Chapter Thirteen
THE CHEEKLINES, THE COMPLEXION, AND MOLES

'There is a garden in her face
Where roses and white lilies blow;
A heavenly paradise is that place,
Wherein all pleasant fruits do flow:
There cherries grow which none may buy
Till "Cherry-ripe" themselves do cry.'

From *Cherry Ripe* by Thomas Campian.

As the face ages it acquires a number of lines or creases, known as wrinkles, which inevitably become more numerous as the years pass, and which are rightly held to reflect the inner changes of character, and the gaining of wisdom, that life's experiences bring. Indeed, the face of a child is normally unmarked by these lines, while that of an old man or woman is often generously, sometimes grotesquely, etched with them.

We have already considered the lines of the forehead, which may appear quite early in life, and also the crow's feet, which arrive later. We must now pay some attention to those that form on the lower part of the face, and which may not develop until age 30 or thereabouts.

The most important of these lines are the two cheeklines, or, as the Chinese call them, the *fa ling*. They start at the upper portion of each of the nostrils' wings, and, in their ideal form, run in a gentle curve down past the mouth to end on the sides of the chin. They should be of equal length, quite deeply cut, and not divided or broken (see Figure 126).

Cheeklines of this type represent long life, a modest degree of success, and the gaining of respect and some authority. Such moderate achievement is perhaps best because it does not excite the envy or jealousy of others, adversely affect the health, or disturb the happi-

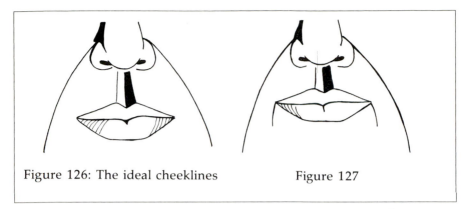

Figure 126: The ideal cheeklines   Figure 127

ness of family life. Hence such cheeklines also portend happiness and contentment, and a possible promotion at either age 55 or 56 or, alternatively, the start of a new phase of life, such as could come about as the result of early retirement.

It is true, however, that well-marked cheeklines occur far more often in men than they do in women. Indeed, many women under the age of 30 show no trace of them at all. This is partly due to the physical differences between a woman's and a man's face—a woman's face, for example, has more subcutaneous fat—but it is primarily a reflection of the fact that until fairly recently few women worked outside the home, which prevented the development of lines that signify success in the world. Yet when a woman is destined to become important and influential, she invariably has them. Three good examples of women who have, or had, prominent cheeklines are Margaret Thatcher (see Figure 61), Golda Meir, and Indira Ghandi.

When deeply marked and unbroken cheeklines reach down well below the level of the mouth, they not only symbolize a successful life but also a long one. If such lines are accompanied by short creases running down from the corners of the mouth (see Figure 127), they signify great success and the attainment of a prominent position in business, art or literature. However, such markings must be partnered by bright, masterful eyes, a fleshy, straight or convex nose, and a strong chin, etc., to make such an analysis certain.

In rare cases long, deeply-cut cheeklines and down-drooping lines from the mouth corners are joined by creases that rise upwards from the chin to the cheeks (see Figure 128). This unique formation, always providing that the other facial features are good, portends great wealth and power, a very high position, and a long life. Thus it is not surprising that only people like monarchs, presidents, and other famous leaders, have such a combination of lines.

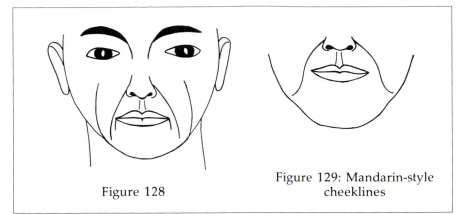

Figure 128

Figure 129: Mandarin-style cheeklines

Long cheeklines sometimes turn outwards at their ends, so giving the face a vaguely Mandarin-type look (see Figure 129). These signify the rise to a high and important position for their owner—in business or finance, or in government service—but not one that brings full power and responsibility.

It is an unfavourable sign when the cheeklines are weakly marked, or broken, or follow a wandering path, as they indicate that the mid-50s will be made unhappy and difficult through ill-health or by unforeseen and unexpected events of a harmful kind. Should either of the cheeklines bear a mole, or a protrusion such as was present on the right cheekline of Abraham Lincoln (see Figure 130), it portends great personal danger at this time: President Lincoln, for example, was shot by an assassin when he was 56.

Cheeklines which are of an unequal length or which follow a dif-

Figure 130: President Abraham Lincoln

ferent course from each other signify an unstable personality and a lack of persistence, which in turn bring disappointment and a failure to attain one's desired goals.

Absent or very short cheeklines in an adult reveal that his, or her, life will end prematurely, i.e. by the age of 56. For example, short cheeklines were possessed by Adolf Hitler (see Figure 92), who shot himself a few days after his 56th birthday, and by Elvis Presley (see Figure 35), who collapsed and died aged 42.

Although it is normally fortunate for the cheeklines to be long and well-marked, their meaning can be compromised by the path they take. If they descend sharply from the wings of the nose, for instance, and pass the mouth in a straight line (see Figure 131), they indicate that the person concerned will bring trouble upon his own head by his way of speaking and by his inability to keep a promise. They also show that he, or she, will suffer from a health breakdown in his middle 50s.

It is very unfortunate when the cheeklines curve inwards and join with the corners of the mouth (see Figure 132), when they portend a premature and rather terrible death, possibly as a result of an accident or by assassination. Yet the Chinese, who call cheeklines of this type 'Dragons Entering the Mouth', say that if the tip of the tongue bears a red mole, it neutralizes the negative effect of the incurving lines and so protects their owner from harm.

The cheeklines also have a negative meaning when they curve upwards from the nose and proceed towards, or end at, the eyes (see Figure 133). Such rarely seen and unusual cheeklines likewise presage an early and tragic death.

The complexion of the face not only either complements or detracts from its beauty, but also reveals a good deal about the owner's health and temperament. The complexion of the face goes hand-in-glove with the quality of the skin. In general, a fine, soft skin is not only more attractive, but also more fortunate in meaning, than one that is thick and coarse. Women naturally have a softer skin than

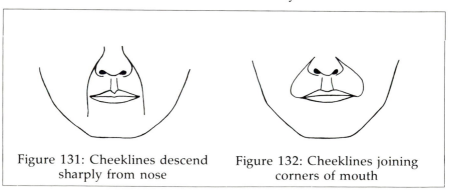

Figure 131: Cheeklines descend   Figure 132: Cheeklines joining
         sharply from nose   corners of mouth

men, although some men are exceptional in this respect. King James I, for example, who was known to his contemporaries as 'the wisest fool in Christendom', was described as having a skin 'as soft as taffeta sarsnet'.

A white, bloodless skin has always been associated with poor health, and one that is habitually pale betokens not only a bad circulation but also a weak heart. Where the character is concerned, a white skin reveals coldness and want of feeling, an unwillingness to become deeply involved with others, and a general lack of direction. It was said of the Roman Emperor Clodius, who was surnamed Albinus because of his remarkably white skin, that 'to his wife he was most hateful, to his slaves unjust, and he was brutal towards the soldiers. Frequently he crucified even centurions on active service, when the nature of the charge did not require it'. This unpleasant man stabbed himself to death on 17 February 197 AD, after having ruled for a little over one year.

The complexion of John Milton was exceedingly fair—he was so fair that they called him 'the Lady of Christ's College', while that of Henry VIII was reported to be 'very fair and bright'. And Plutarch tells us that Alexander the Great 'was fair, with a tinge of red in his face and upon his breast'.

A skin that is pink, with perhaps a heightened redness on the cheeks, is best, as it signifies a lively, cheerful, warm, and unselfish character, and good health. Sir Thomas More, that man for all seasons, had such a skin. 'He has a fair skin, glowing rather than pale,' noted Erasmus, 'though far from ruddy, but a faint rosiness shining through.' So also did Lady Venetia Digby. 'The colour of her cheeks was just about that of a damask rose,' observed John Aubrey, 'which is neither too hot nor too pale.' But her health was not as strong as her complexion suggests. Lady Digby died at age 33.

A complexion which is red rather than pink belongs to the person who is naturally strong in body and energetic, and who has plenty of dash, courage and fire. He is thus extroverted, with a love of com-

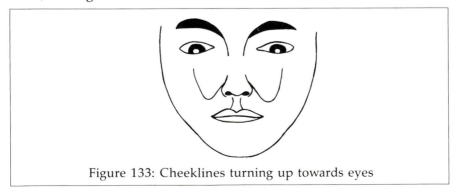

Figure 133: Cheeklines turning up towards eyes

pany and having a good time, and sexually active. Yet his temper is
quick, so making him rather unstable and volatile, and he can be dangerous when crossed or when he drinks heavily.

'His countenance was swollen and reddish,' observed Sir Philip
Warwick of Oliver Cromwell, and we have already mentioned that
the poet and courtier Sir John Suckling, who committed suicide, was
not only 'reddish-faced' but had 'a red nose'. The emperor Domitian
also had a florid face, as did the philosopher Thomas Hobbes, of
whom it was said: 'From forty, or better, he grew healthier, and then
he had a fresh, ruddy complexion . . . his skin was soft.' And the poet
and diplomat Andrew Marvell (see Figure 134), 'was of middling
stature, pretty strong set, roundish-faced, cherry cheeked, hazel eye,
brown hair'. It was he, in his poem titled *To His Coy Mistress*, who
advised:

> 'Now therefore, while the youthful hue
> Sits on thy skin like morning dew,
> And while thy willing soul transpires
> At every pore with instant fires,
> Now let us sport us while we may,
> And now, like amorous birds of prey,
> Rather at once our time devour
> Than languish in his slow-chapt power.
> Let us roll all our strength and all
> Our sweetness up into one ball,
> And tear our pleasures with rough strife
> Thorough the iron gates of life:
> Thus, though we cannot make our sun
> Stand still, yet we will make him run.'

When blueness appears in the face it is a sign of poor circulation,
which may be due to a cardiac or renal insufficiency, and hence is
indicative of poor health. Those with a bluish complexion lack
energy and vitality, are often sickly, and have trouble achieving their
goals. Blue spots must also be regarded as negative influences on the
age point where they occur, and presage either ill-health, misfortune,
or a loss of position, at that time. Any extensive blueness of the face
can indicate an early death.

A yellow complexion, or a face that is yellow in places, was once
believed to have been caused by a surfeit of yellow bile, which gave
to those with this colour a rather bitter, warped, irritable, and gloomy
personality. And such a view, old though it is, is not entirely wrong,
as the yellow-faced do tend to be introverted, narrow-minded, and
pessimistic. Yellowness is likewise an indicator of health problems
like gout and rheumatism, or if the colour is found only in the whites
of the eyes, of more serious conditions like diabetes. When a yellow

Figure 134: Andrew Marvell (1621–1678)

complexion accompanies negative facial features such as cold eyes, a bony aquiline nose, and thin lips, it signifies a person who is selfish, proud and cruel.

The Greeks of pre-Classical times frequently named their children according to the shape or colour of their faces, and indeed some of the most attractive names from their mythology turn out to be nothing more than facial descriptions. The name Europe, for example, given to the daughter of Agenor and Telephassa, means 'broad face', and was once a title of the moon. Other names with a heavenly connection include Sinope or 'moon-face', Asterope or 'star-face', and Aerope or 'sky-face'. Names which derive more from the face's colouring than its likeness to a celestial object or region, are Leirope or 'lily face', Oenope or 'wine face', Pelopia or 'muddy face', and Calliope or 'fair face', while Sterope or 'stubborn face' and Gorgopis or 'grim-faced', clearly refer to the expression rather than the face's shape or complexion. Only a few ancient Greek names capture the form of particular facial parts, such as Eriopis or 'large-eyed' and Simoeis or 'snub-nosed', although the most famous Greek hero, Achilles, was obviously distinguished by the thinness of his lips, as his name means 'lipless'. Thin lips can presage an early death, and Achilles was killed by an arrow shot into his vulnerable heel, when he was between 25 and 30 years of age (in 1184 BC).

Moles are found on the face in a variety of shapes, sizes, colours, and numbers. However, their most important quality is their shine or radiance. Radiant moles, particularly if they are black or red in colour, are lucky and so augment the facial part on which they occur. Dull moles, on the other hand, especially if they are grey or brown in colour, are unlucky and thus compromise the place where they lie.

A face that is entirely free of moles betokens an absence of inner sparkle and indicates that the person's life will not be helped along by any lucky breaks, whereas the presence of many dull moles is a sign of inner conflict, and shows that the person concerned will have difficulty in coming to terms with his limitations and with the setbacks in life that he (or she) will inevitably experience.

A mole's effects can be dated by its position. A mole (or moles) on the forehead, for example, relates to events that take place in its owner's middle to late teens and 20s, while a mole on the nose refers to happenings in his, or her, 40s.

A mole should ideally be round in shape, when it is also considered lucky. A round mole emphasizes the good points of the part in question, while at the same time having a specific meaning relating to its position. Misshapen moles are unlucky; they can indicate a person struggling with conflicting desires. Oblong moles are often symbolic of financial gain, yet this has to be worked for.

Moles should be neither too large nor too small. Moles are considered large when they exceed one eighth of an inch in diameter. Large moles indicate coarseness and an overdevelopment of the character traits signified by the facial part or area on which they lie, to the extent that they become harmful. Small moles, that is, moles which are under one-sixteenth of an inch in diameter, are representative of qualities or attributes that have not been fully developed. Small moles in certain areas of the face suggest a cramped, narrow outlook.

Thus, in general, a round, dark or red radiant mole of modest size is the ideal type of mole to have.

If you have fortunate moles on your chin you are tolerant and affectionate, and you are open in your dealings with others. You enjoy travel and new sights, although you are not so welcoming of new ideas. If your other features are confirmatory, you are a responsible, hard working employee, a good friend, and are (or will be) a kind and loving parent. If your chin moles are oblong in shape, they reveal that you have a calculating streak in your nature.

Lip moles must be assessed carefully. The lips are sensual areas and the presence of moles on them always indicates a tendency towards warmth, passion, and animal enjoyment. If you have round, fortunate moles on your lips, you are open, loving and demonstrative in your affections. A dull or misshapen mole (or moles), however, shows you to be overly passionate; if this is also grey or brown in colour, your sexual needs are very intense and thus somewhat problematical.

If you have moles on your cheeks they reveal that you have intellectual interests and that you are also somewhat withdrawn. You are therefore fascinated by ideas and by any intellectual challenge. Yet because you are unable to respond warmly to others, you will often feel lonely and isolated. You are not greatly interested in material possessions. Indeed, the treasures of the mind are far more important to you.

Should you have a mole at the outside corner of one or other of your eyes, it signifies that you are a straightforward, honest person, although you are too easily influenced by the opinions of others. But should this mole be dull, or misshapen, or grey or brown in colour, or show all three traits, then your integrity is compromised and you may become a yes-man.

Laziness and selfishness are symbolized by an unfortunate mole appearing above the left eyebrow. If you have such a mole you may suffer much hardship because of these deficiencies of character.

It is never lucky to have a mole on the eyelids, as it is the mark of a person who has talent but who is unable to utilize this talent fully. However, the meaning of this mole is enhanced if a balancing mole appears on the chin, where it signifies stronger and more purposeful character traits.

A fortunate mole appearing in or above the right eyebrow is very lucky. It augurs considerable success after years of struggle, the key to which is the person's determination and refusal to give in, no matter how great the odds.

When a fortunate mole is present on the lobe of the ear, it signifies a wise mind and an interest in spiritual pursuits. But an unfortunate mole on the ear lobe—that is, one that is dull, misshapen and grey or brown in colour—shows that its owner will use his knowledge for personal gain.

Moles appearing anywhere on the ears except the lobes are indicative of wealth, hence those possessing them will never have to worry about money. Large moles portend great wealth, small moles suggest a more modest fortune. But while radiant, round red or black moles reveal that the gains will be acquired honestly or may perhaps be inherited, dull, misshapen grey or brown moles indicate that they will be obtained through dishonest activities or possibly by theft.

When a mole lies on the bridge of the nose between the eyebrows, it signifies a changeable career pattern and a difficulty in settling down; a high position will therefore elude its owner until perhaps late in life. A lucky mole, however, symbolizes some fortunate return from the changes, whereas an unlucky mole reveals that they will be the cause of much bitterness and unhappiness.

A mole on the bridge of the nose between the eyes is an unlucky sign, even though it might be of the 'fortunate' variety. Such a mole presages marital problems and the likelihood of a divorce; it also warns of a major health breakdown. A fortunate mole, however, suggests that these events will be far less traumatic than they might otherwise have been, while a dull and misshapen mole reveals acrimony and upset, although it has to be read with regard to the rest of the face to determine if these are short-lived disturbances or if their occurrence throws a shadow over the life.

Lastly, it can be mentioned that a mole sited in the philtrum of a man is one warning that he will die prematurely; however, should such a mole be found in the philtrum of a woman it shows that she will suffer from gynaecological problems, which may make her infertile.

AFTERWORD

There is no such thing as a perfect face, for that could only be possessed by someone with a perfect character, health and fate, whatever they may be. I have, however, on numerous occasions in the previous pages referred to 'ideal' features, by which I mean those signifying the best of the qualities linked with them. A perfect face, I suppose, would be formed entirely of ideal features, and would belong to some god-like being who could not really exist. For even the most admired and respected of people, like Socrates, St. Joan and Jesus Christ, had traits of character and ways of behaving that made them enemies, which is why Socrates was forced to drink hemlock, St. Joan was burned at the stake, and Christ was crucified. Their faces must therefore have borne signs of their difficulties with their fellows and of their premature and violent deaths, and hence could not have been perfect. Thus don't be too upset if your own face is flawed in some way, as you are not alone.

But do remember, however, that your own or anyone else's face can only be accurately interpreted by combining the meanings of all of its parts, by weighing those features that are good against those that are bad and extracting the balance of truth from them. This is not an easy task, and you are advised to proceed slowly and carefully. Be aware that one inferior or flawed feature can be salvaged to some extent by another or others which is or are better formed, or by its bright colour, good skin, radiant moles, etc. And even if a feature suggests a lack of worldly success at the time of life with which it is associated, ask yourself if such success would really bring you happiness if you achieved it? For it is happiness that people are seeking when they hunger after money, power and fame, although such things rarely, if ever, provide it.

That being so, I'll leave you with some more thoughts of John

Ruskin, with whose ideas on man's business in life I began this book. He wrote:

'To watch the corn grow and the blossoms set; to draw hard breath over ploughshare or spade; to read, to think, to love, to hope, to pray—these are the things that make men happy; they always had the power of doing these things; they never will have power to do more. The world's prosperity or adversity depends upon our knowing and teaching these few things.'

INDEX

Of further interest . . .

FORTUNE-TELLING BY PALMISTRY

A Practical Guide to the Art of Hand Analysis

RODNEY DAVIES

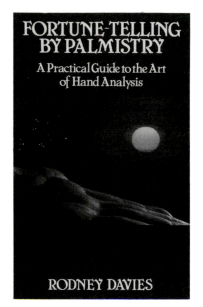

Palmistry is an ancient method of character analysis and divination that has always aroused great interest. Modern scientific investigation has conclusively shown that the hands are the living symbols of an individual's health, character and psychological state.

This up-to-date and informative book shows how to read your hands to reveal your prospects in love, work, money and happiness.

Contents include:
★ the hand and the planets
★ hand shape and character
★ the wearing of rings
★ fortunate signs and markings
★ the changing hands